Aeschylus

...gave expression to the imagination and ideals that marked his epoch as the Golden Age of Greece.

Athens had conquered tyranny and was a flourishing democracy. In this center of politics and culture men engendered concepts of humanity that were to become our everlasting heritage.

Through such plays as Prometheus Bound, *through the use of myth and legend, the great tragic dramatist illustrated a new vision – a vision of human destiny and divine purpose.*

Prometheus, condemned to hideous suffering because he dared to wrest fire from the gods and give it to man, has become the eternal symbol of human progress and enlightenment. This brilliant new translation of Aeschylus' classic work reveals the noble tragedy of that divine ordeal.

The Theater at Epidauros

Slide #31 from the Raymond V. Schoder, S. J. series, © 1987 Bolchazy-Carducci Publishers, Inc.

A E S C H Y L U S
PROMETHEUS BOUND

A New Translation, Introduction, Commentary
Paul Roche

Illustrations by
Thom Kapheim

Bolchazy-Carducci Publishers, Inc.
Wauconda, Illinois
1998

The Greek text used throughout is (with an occasional exception) that published by the Loeb Classical Library. This is the text established by Herbert Weir Smyth, basing himself on the Medicean ms. written about 1000.

Published by
Bolchazy-Carducci Publishers, Inc
1000 Brown Street, Wauconda, Illinois 60084
http://www.bolchazy.com

ISBN: 0-86516-238-7

Reprint of the 1964 Mentor Classics Edition

Printed in the United States of America
1998
by United Graphics

Library of Congress Cataloging-in-Publication Data

Roche, Paul, 1927-
   Aeschylus : Prometheus bound / a new translation, introduction,
commentary, Paul Roche ; illustrations by Thom Kapheim.
   128 p. : ill. : 23 cm.
   ISBN 0-86516-238-7
   I. Title. II. Title: Prometheus bound.
MLCM 92/08661 (P)   90-177320

ΑΙΣΧΥΛΟΥ

ΠΡΟΜΗΘΕΥΣ ΔΕΣΜΩΤΗΣ

ΧΘΟΝΟΣ ΜΕΝ ΕΣ ΤΗΛΟΥΡΟΝ ΗΚΟΜΕΝ ΠΕΔΟΝ

ΣΚΥΘΗΝ ΕΣ ΟΙΜΟΝ ΑΒΑΤΟΝ ΕΙΣ ΕΡΗΜΙΑΝ

ΗΦΑΙΣΤΕ ΣΟΙ ΔΕ ΧΡΗ ΜΕΛΕΙΝ ΕΠΙΣΤΟΛΑΣ

ΑΣ ΣΟΙ ΠΑΤΗΡ ΕΦΕΙΤΟ ΤΟΝΔΕ ΠΡΟΣ ΠΕΤΡΑΙΣ

ΥΨΗΛΟΚΡΗΜΝΟΙΣ ΤΟΝ ΛΕΩΡΓΟΝ ΟΧΜΑΣΑΙ

ΑΔΑΜΑΝΤΙΝΩΝ ΔΕΣΜΩΝ ΕΝ ΑΡΡΗΚΤΟΙΣ ΠΕΔΑΙΣ

for KIMON FRIAR
homage within the great tradition

κἀι παρ' Ἑλλήνων τινές
ἴτων πάλῳ λαχόντες ὡς νομίζεται.
μαντεύομαι γὰρ ὡς ἂν ἡγῆται θεός.

(Let any Greeks here enter in by lot
      according to the law,
and I shall prophesy as the god leads on.)
                        The Eumenides 31-33

Slices from Homer's mighty dinners

            (Aeschylus, of his own works:
                  Athenaeus 8.347 e)

CONTENTS

INTRODUCTION

I THE EVOLUTION OF STATURE, HUMAN AND DIVINE

The conflict in Greek tragedy, as in life, is bifurcated and ambivalent. It is not that one action is good and another bad, but that the goodness is often fraught with badness and the bad with good. Unbridled self-assertion *(hybris)* does not merely lead to sin—it is already sin. And yet unbridled self-assertion against tyranny is glorious—a cause for martyrdom.

In *Prometheus Bound* we have two symbols pitted against each other. One represents the free spirit of human progress, the other the uncompromising pressure of preterhuman sanctions whether of religion or tradition. It is in their cross encounter that a synthesis, a reconciliation, is achieved.

The stand of Prometheus against Zeus, in so far as it is a stand against arbitrary power, is splendid. Insofar as it is merely personal defiance of eternal principalities it is rash, even fatuous. Insofar as it is a testament of faith and a manifesto in which Prometheus himself willingly accepts his role as "vessel of dishonor" and allows himself to become the receptacle of divine wrath because of what he has done, it is holy.

The "holy sinner" becomes the prime mover in this dialectic of human development. He is even more: the catalyst in the evolving concept of deity itself. For there can be no real progress until the anthropomorphic props of religious fundamentalism themselves merge into theology and become synthesized in turn with an expanding consciousness.

The point of the Promethean trilogy (of which this play is the only extant member) is to show us two grand and intransigent impulses in mutual clash and defiance. Since they are both eternal and cannot destroy one another, the conflict threatens to harden into a painful and appalling deadlock unless one or other modifies itself and enters into a new relationship. Aeschylus demonstrates that it is precisely in a compromise, in the grinding of opposing principles toward a synthesis, that not loss but growth and abiding stature are to be found. In a sense Prometheus is suffering for mankind, and in a sense man himself is being tried: his defiance and his defenselessness. One is to prove the eternal justification of kindness and saving intelligence over brute compulsion; the other is to be transmuted into a noble partnership.

Attendant on this major lesson are others. Each antagonist represents both the good and the bad. Prometheus is enlightenment and the progressive spirit of humanity. He is also—though a god—the spirit of unbridled delinquency and self-assertion. Zeus is ultimate law, order and religion: the moral basis of the universe. He is also primitive vindictiveness, unthinking legalism and crass despotism. All these elements are to work upon one another— thesis and antithesis struggling within a mutual alchemy—to produce the correction and the new direction in which all things must go forward.

Even within the confines and conventions of Greek drama Aeschylus speaks with a living and a timely voice. The whole orientation of the modern world, with its discovery of space—which is itself the symbol of the removal of finite boundaries to its theology—falls without a jar into the incredible loftiness and propinquity of Aeschylus's own teleology. But apart from this he has a more immediate message still. Life, whether through our own mistakes or those of others, has a tragic cast to it and we must suffer. It is important for us to realize that that suffering need not be nugatory or prolonged. Everything that happens to us is a process: good, bad and indifferent. It is up to us to accept this positively and by purifying our motives and our consciousness to make it also a progress. We cannot arrange the circumstances, the impulses, the patterns of life into which we were born. We *can* arrange their organization and the degree of completion to which we push them. Progress is painful, but progress is also exhilarating. We should always be developing, enlarging: freeing our virtues from self-righteousness—from the catastrophe that always overtakes arrogance—and merging them into something more cooperative and loving. We must move toward an expansion of vision: into the full view of the pain and the glory of being human; but it must be in terms of something greater than the human. Through all the unperceived laminations of matter and spirit, through the hidden peripheries of a constant but intangible contact, there must emerge some sort of juncture of the human with the divine as a natural fact of creation, not as an extra. From it immediately flows a luminous recognition of the sheer scope and clemency of existence in spite of its ruthlessness (call it Fate if you like) wherein everything falls into place, where we and all things impinge on all things—on divinity itself—and where nothing is wasted.

Such are the ideals symbolically adumbrated in

the *Prometheia*. They are propagated movingly
and by way of art, not by preaching or propa-
ganda. Unfortunately, Aeschylus takes us only to
the first stage of his dialectic in this play. We may
surmise however from every evidence internal and
external that he works it out to its conclusion in
the two lost plays that went with it—as he does in
another way in his *Oresteia*. We need not con-
sciously be thinking of these things as we read or
act *Prometheus Bound*. It is enough to move along
with the sublime and sonorous language and to
feel both the vehemence and the sweetness of the
story.

II THE PLAY AND THE AUTHOR

Out of some ninety plays from the hand of
Aeschylus *Prometheus Bound* is one of the only
seven that have come down to us. It is almost un-
doubtedly the second part of a trilogy of which
the first part was *Prometheus the Fire-Bringer*, and
the last, *Prometheus Unbound*. It must have been
produced about 465 B.C. Aeschylus was then sixty.
Ten years of his noble, independent, and varied
life were left to him. He had fought as a soldier in
three great battles. He had been a man of affairs.
He had established himself as the master tragic poet
of his time. Some ten years earlier he had paid the
first of his visits to Sicily, receiving from his en-
lightened patron, King Hiero, the reward of fame.
He was to be spared from seeing that same Sicily
gratuitously attacked by his own Athens a generation or so later and the flower of the Attic army destroyed or crowded to their deaths in the stone
quarries of Epipolai. Six years after the production

of the Prometheus trilogy, and closely following the victory of his *Oresteia* in the tragedy competitions, he was to go to Sicily again, there to die in 455 B.C., a playwright for forty-five years and the prize winner thirteen times.

If in any sense ancient Greece may be said to have witnessed an Elizabethan age, the age of Pericles was surely it, and Aeschylus lived through the heart of it—its Shakespeare or its Marlowe. Even if such analogies are dangerous, because they suggest a series of affinities which are not parallel, it remains true that Aeschylus par excellence embodied the spirit of imagination and expansion that signalized his epoch. Athens had blossomed from tyranthood into democracy, the invading Persian hordes had been broken and dispersed, the city itself had become the political and cultural center of Greece. Men whom common danger had drawn together now shared a new impulse toward liberty, justice, and spiritual unity: those grand ideals to which Aeschylus was to give magnificent expression in his plays.

In the myths and legends of the race he discovered an ethical and religious content: he transformed them into problems of human destiny or of the divine righteousness: Prometheus suffers, Io suffers, before our eyes; and instantly we are made to confront the question whether the lord of Olympus is a just god. He naturalized himself in those high altitudes of thought and emotion whence he could survey the springs of good and evil, the mysterious agencies of the fate that makes man's character its instrument, the relation of punishment to sin, the meaning of suffering, the dealings of God with man, and the essential unity of the divine purpose.[1]

This last was his highest contribution to thought. He demonstrated a new principle: he took the gods and goddesses of Mount Olympus, recognized the validity of what they stood for, scoured them of the dross of merely human association, and merged their function and their purpose into a total concept of deity which was transcendent, universal, inescapably operative, and (for the first time) one with Fate.

III THE SEQUEL TO THE STORY

Prometheus Bound ends with a gigantic terrestrial upheaval—storm and thunderbolts—and Prometheus, together with the rock to which he is chained, sinks into Hades.

Piecing together what we know from various sources and from extant fragments of the *Prometheus Unbound,* the rest of the story as Aeschylus unfolded it goes something like this:

After the lapse of thirty thousand years, Prometheus reemerges into the light, but is fastened to Mount Caucasus, where he is visited daily by the eagle that gluts on his liver. He is to remain in this plight until some other immortal is willing to take his place in Hades. At last Heracles (Io's descendant and the promised "man mighty with the bow") comes upon Prometheus in his journey to the Hesperides. He shoots the eagle and persuades Chiron, the wise Centaur—who has been incurably wounded by a poisoned arrow—to descend into Hades instead of Prometheus. Chiron, to escape the

[1] Herbert Weir Smyth, in the Introduction to his text and translation of the plays of Aeschylus.

unbearable pain, is ready to renounce his immortality. Prometheus then reveals the name of the goddess (Thetis) who will "bear a son mightier than the sire," to Zeus's overthrow, if he marries her. At last he is set free, but as a reminder of his punishment he wears forever afterwards an iron ring on his finger and a crown of willow leaves on his head. He is reinstated on Olympus and becomes once again the prophet and adviser of the gods, thus symbolizing the fact that the wisdom he embodied has eternally passed into the soul of Zeus. On earth his name is perpetually honored as the founder and savior of human civilization, and at Athens as a minor deity he shares a common altar with Hephaestus, god of fire.

IV A TRANSLATOR'S ADMISSIONS

I have spoken at perhaps too great length elsewhere[2] of the problems that beset the translator of Greek tragedy. Let me mention here only that the problem for me remains a poetic problem, which is to say, primarily a problem of sound. In short, how does one create and organize a pattern of sound, cadence, and rhythm which will have an emotive effect in one's own tongue parallel to that which it has in the Greek?

Apprenticed first to Sophocles, developing my technique through an intensive course with Aeschylus, I thought I had devised a method which caught at least the beginnings of what was wanted. It consisted in fixing one's model with a passionate observance and trying not to imitate him meta-

[2] *The Oedipus Plays of Sophocles, The Orestes Plays of Aeschylus.* New York: The New American Library.

phrastically but, as far as possible to re-create, that is, transpose into English, as many qualities as could be shared without strain by both languages.

I had a horror of what seemed to me the three mistakes in handling[8] Greek drama: the overloaded pseudo-Swinburnian, the dead-beat, tone-deaf, honest-to-goodness academic, and the attempt (doomed from the start) to make English sound like Greek.

As to the first and second, Mount Parnassus was out, yes, but so was an exaggerated fear of it. As to the last: English cannot take a photograph of Greek. One language best translates another when it is least like it and most like itself.

In my preface to *The Oedipus Plays of Sophocles* I wrote:

> I have been careful to watch Sophocles. Where he has repeated a word, *I* have repeated it; where he is rich in assonance and alliteration, I try to be; where he is harsh and staccato, I try to catch it; where he has a ringing tone, I try to ring. I have tried to walk and to run, to rise and to sit, with the master, but never by imitation, only by analogy, transposition and re-creation.

That was all very well, but when it came to the *Prometheus* and I began to put my method to the test again after what had seemed to me a successful run with the *Oresteia*, I realized after about six hundred lines that something was not quite right. No matter how I watched him, the Grand Old Man of Greek tragedy was eluding me. With all my passionate observance, I could not seem to strike a spark from him. It was like looking at some supposedly excellent film which, for some reason

[8] I am speaking here of strict translation, not of mere paraphrase, adaptation, or "imitation."

one could not tell, remained (or became) plain dull.

Then an obvious thing struck me. The *Prometheus* was pure ideolyrical drama—one of the best examples of it: a drama of ideas in which the dramatic content was small but the epic singing voice strong, and the whole produced within a tightly organized pattern of sound. I saw that the unity between the chorus and the actors was complete and the plot so simple that it had to be carried by something more than dramatic action. With the hero himself chained to a rock throughout, and none of the characters undergoing any change, so little happened in this drama of grand ideas that not to treat it almost as a kind of oratorio was to mistake its identity. In other words, it was the sheer verbal music in the *Prometheus* that created the pace, the interest, the emotion. Even the tedious litany of place names in Io's wanderings was made fascinating by its incantation and sonority.

I looked at my efforts again. The verbal music was at least as strong as I had made it in the *Agamemnon*, but then the *Agamemnon* was five times as dramatic. I opened Elizabeth Barrett Browning's beautiful version. Next to hers mine seemed like pages torn from the telephone directory. But I could not do what she had done to get the sound. Her rendering is too romantic and too wordy to capture the Greek in its un-English and miraculous marriage of grandiloquence with despatch. I looked at Aeschylus again, hardly expecting to find more than what I already knew: namely, that his style was rich indeed—pegged and wedged and dovetailed with assonance, consonance, alliteration, and even rhyme.

Then something else struck me; something so

obvious that no scholar had ever bothered to tell me: ninety-five per cent of the line endings in the *Prometheus* are "tied-up." I mean by this rough-and-ready phrase that Aeschylus, using all the poetic amenities of an inflected language (many of them no doubt fortuitous to his purpose), inter-relates by a system of consonance and half-con-sonance, of rhyme and half-rhyme—often throw-ing in end assonance as well—the end syllables of the vast majority of his lines. These analogies of sound do not of course fall with the same strength as they do in English, because they do not always fall on the accented syllable of words, and the words are much longer than in English. Neverthe-less, by this device each eи.d syllable is turned into a small coping stone or cornice neatly finishing off an already heavily caparisoned latticework of ver-bal music. I saw at once that this coping stone not only helped to trim the sometimes almost rampant luxury of beautiful sounds within a line, by steady-ing it, but it also built the line into the solid edifice of the whole passage by relating it sonically to all the others.[4]

This was an exciting discovery indeed. The question now was: Could the same thing be done in English? Was there any approximation to that combination of spontaneity and formality? Look-ing again at my six hundred abortive lines, I saw that on the occasions when I had come anywhere near to the emotive force in Aeschylus, I had in fact without realizing it "tied-up" my line ends. All I had to do now was to work at this con-sciously and more or less systematically.[5]

[4] I give two illustrations of this in the appendix.

[5] The word "system" is a dangerous word. No good trans-lation, let alone good poetry, has ever been produced by means of a system. The conscious mind lets through only what it

I knew I could keep a steady eye on Aeschylus, watching to see when and how and why he interlaced his end syllables. Of course, if the thing were pushed too far, made into a fetish or a formula, it would ruin everything. The line endings must not be too strong—though they would of necessity be stronger than in the Greek—and they must above all give the appearance of falling naturally, almost by accident. What was wanted was something between the cohesion and formality of the heroic couplet and the naturalness of blank verse.

I redid my six hundred lines. The changes sometimes seemed scarcely detectable, but their effect— at least on me—was immediate. I no longer had the feeling when I read the thing aloud that I was viewing a supposedly excellent film every shot of which took just three seconds too long. . . . Be that as it may. What intrigued me in the effort was that in it I pushed my principles to an extreme. The result I must leave to others to judge. My own hope is that certain associations of sound and rhythm have been given a new emphasis: one which will have a value, if only for me, in the writing of fresh poetry.

If there is anything left to say about a work which purports to be strictly faithful to the original, I think it is this: two qualities of Aeschylus must above all be kept in translation. One is the quasi-liturgical solemnity of his utterance. More than Sophocles, much more than Euripides, Aeschylus hews to the semihieratic mission of Greek tragedy. He is dealing with more than ordinary people. They do not speak ordinary language—

knows—and what it knows is only a fraction of what it circumscribes. Formulas, *per necessità*, are sieves, which let through reality only by excluding the bulk of it.

or at least they heighten it. . . . The other is: distance. We cannot and must not try to make *Prometheus* contemporary. His own basic universality makes him that. There are two distances for the translator to keep: *our* distance from Aeschylus; his own from Homer, who provided him with characters and events from an age of heroes and pre-heroes many hundreds of years anterior to his own.

Paul Roche

Aldermaston
March 1964

V TIME AND SETTING

It is the heroic age of prehistory. Three figures move across a desolate landscape high above the sea. A fourth is led along behind them. He is aloof, unresisting, and impassively noble. Such is Prometheus the fallen Titan, who helped Zeus to his throne and then incurred his anger. His name means "Forethought" or "Providence." Having been responsible for the creation of mankind, he countered Zeus's neglect of men by giving them stolen fire from heaven. He continued in his determination to educate, develop, and help them in the face of the god's resentment and wish to wipe away the lot. For the new ruler of the gods seems to prefer the old orthodox safety of man's ignorance and subservience to knowledge and progress. Prometheus is being taken to the scene of his vindictive punishment. It is a vast stage in both space and time. The party comes to a rugged cleft in the mountainside and halts.

PROMETHEUS
BOUND

THE CHARACTERS

MIGHT

FORCE

HEPHAESTUS: god of fire and the forge

PROMETHEUS: fallen Titan

CHORUS: of Oceanids—daughters of OCEAN

OCEAN: a Titan, god of seas and rivers

IO: daughter of INACHUS

HERMES: messenger of ZEUS

PROMETHEUS
BOUND

MIGHT

We've come to the end, then—the world's end:
This Scythian tract, a desert without men.[1]
Here, Hephaestus, you must now despatch
That mandate which the Father laid on you
And clamp this rebel to the crag-capt rocks
With adamantine bonds that none can break.
Your very flower, your fire, the spark of artifex,
He filched and gave to mortal man.
    Such his sin,
For which he has to pay the gods and learn
Respect for Zeus's sovereignty
And cease his philanthropic turn.

HEPHAESTUS

Yes, Might and Force,
The task Zeus gave you is complete
And nothing keeps you here,

[1] I take the reading ἄβροτον ("without mortals") rather than that of ἄβχτον ("untrodden").

But as for me I have no heart
To bind by force a fellow god
Upon this winter-riven scar
And I must summon all my strength for it:
There's danger in the Father disobeyed.
  Prometheus, soaring-minded son
Of Themis, queen of thinking right,
Against your will and mine,
Indissolubly fettered must I nail you to this crag
Remote from man;
Where no voice, no human form shall meet your
                                        sight,
But, burning in the sun's bright heat,
Your flesh shall lose its flower
And glad you'll be when jeweled night
Veils from you the glare,
And glad when the morning sun
Breaks up again the rime.
Ages shall pass of this present wasting pain,
For he who comes to ease you is not born.

MIGHT

Well, why do you wait? Why sympathize in
                                        vain,
And do not hate the god whom all the gods must
                                        hate:
The one who sold your birthright to mankind?

HEPHAESTUS

There's something strange in kin and fellowship.

HEPHAESTUS

Indissolubly fettered must I nail you to this crag
Remote from man. . .

MIGHT

So I grant, and yet to flout the Father's words—
is that possible? Isn't that more strange than anything?

HEPHAESTUS

Always so pitiless and so uncurbed!

MIGHT

Certainly, when crying for *him* cannot cure a
thing.
Don't waste your time on something so in vain.

HEPHAESTUS

How I now detest my craftsmanship!

MIGHT
Why loathe that, when in literal truth
you cannot curse your craft for present pain?

HEPHAESTUS

Nevertheless, I wish it were another's lot.

MIGHT

All roles are hard, except to rule in heaven:
none alive is free but Zeus alone.

HEPHAESTUS

I know it, and I cannot contradict.

MIGHT

Hurry, then, and cast him round with fetters;
not let the Father catch you loitering.

HEPHAESTUS

Of course, of course! The manacles are ready.

MIGHT

Then clap them on his wrists
and rock the mallet with a mighty swing
to peg him to the crags.
                    [HEPHAESTUS *exerts himself*]

HEPHAESTUS

The job is done; it is not shoddy work.

MIGHT

Hit harder. Grapple him. Leave nothing loose.
He's terrible: finds chinks in the impossible.

HEPHAESTUS

This arm at least is pinned beyond his wits.

MIGHT

Then clamp the other fast and let him learn,
clever though he is, that next to Zeus he lags.

HEPHAESTUS

There!—None but he could justly find a fault.

MIGHT

Now, right through his chest with a lusty stroke,
drive the steely and unfeeling stake.

HEPHAESTUS

My poor Prometheus, how I groan for you!

MIGHT

What! Hanging back again?
Groans for Zeus's enemies?
Take care your pity's not needed for your own.

HEPHAESTUS

A sight for sore eyes—the spectacle you see.

MIGHT

What I see is someone getting his desserts.
Come on; clinch those bands around his sides.

HEPHAESTUS

Of course—I must. Stop ordering me.

MIGHT

I'll order you, and press you to exert

yourself; get down there and ring his legs by force.
[HEPHAESTUS *stoops and places the*
manacles round PROMETHEUS's *feet*]

HEPHAESTUS

So . . . that job is done. And not long doing it.

MIGHT

Now with a swing, strike those keen fetters
home.
We have a hard and ruthless overseer.

HEPHAESTUS

Your tongue's as brutal as your body.

MIGHT

You can play the weakling—but don't you dare
throw insults at my strength of will and solid ire.

HEPHAESTUS

Then, let us go. Now that he is utterly en-
meshed.
[*Exit* HEPHAESTUS, *leaving* MIGHT *and* FORCE,
who stand jeering at the silent PROMETHEUS]

MIGHT

Ha! Be superior now.
Go snatch the perquisites of deity
And hand them to ephemerals.
Will they ease—these mortals—

One single of your pains?
Prometheus, "Man of Forethought"! Ha!
Misnomer of the gods it was, and you misnamed.
You need your own forethinker now to pry you
                                                    free.
                    [*Exeunt* MIGHT *and* FORCE]

PROMETHEUS

Come, sweet celestial space
    and quick-winged airs,

Come, springing streams
    and deep-sea-dimpled seas
        in crinkled laugh;

Come, mother-of-all, great Earth,
    and round all-staring sun—
I call on you to see my hurt:
    a god's but done by gods.

Gaze upon my mangled wrestling,
    my millennium of pain to come.
        Disgrace and chains

The new Commander of the Blessed
    puts on me. . . .
        O I cry, cry

For sorrows here and those to come.
For where or when is destined ever
    a close to all these pains?

But what do I say?
When every item of the future I foresee

And nothing of my agony can come as a surprise.
No, I must bear my fate as best I may,
Knowing that nothing can resist the force of what
                                        must be.
To talk or not to talk about my state
Is equally impossible;
And after all my benisons to men
Here I am caught beneath this yoke—compelled:
I the one who snared within a fennel stalk
The source of fire—
Man's great teacher of the arts, his universal boon.
This is the sin for which I pay the price,
Clamped beneath the naked sky and shackled here.
                    [*There is a stir in the air like
                        the distant sound of wings*]

    Ah! What now?
A sound, a wafted scent—intangible—
Heavenly or human or between?
Does someone come to spy upon my struggles
Here at this verge of all, this peak . . .
Or wanting what?

    Come look upon this bitter god in fetters:
Enemy of Zeus, detested by the lot
Of gods that go to Zeus's court;
And all because I was a friend too much of man.
                            [*The sound is nearer*]

    Ah, there again!
That rushing past my ears—of birds?
Faint whistle of air and stir—of wings?
Everything that comes to me is full of fear.
            [*The* CHORUS *of sea-nymphs, daughters of
            Oceanus, enter on a winged chariot, from
            which they sing compassionately to* PROME-
                                        THEUS]

CHORUS Strophe 1

So I winged on my chariot; sped without sandals.

CHORUS
Strophe 1

Be not afraid, for in fondness
And racing as rivals on pinions
This troupe with consent of their father
(Grudgingly won) is arriving
Here on this peak; and the breezes
Carry me swiftly toward you.
For the clang and the echo of iron
Drove through our innermost cavern
Striking the look of sweet calm from our eyes;
So I winged on my chariot; sped without sandals.

PROMETHEUS

Aah! Aah!
Offspring of Tethys that many-child mother,
Children of him who on every shore
Rolls round the earth his unslumbering waters
    (Ocean, your father):
    Observe me and gaze at the fetters
    That coop me so high to this fanged
        Chasm, to keep
    My undesirable stand.

CHORUS
Antistrophe 1

I see you, Prometheus. Fear
Spreads in a mist through my eyes
At the sight of your body in bonds,
Withering away in disgrace,
Locked in steel on this rock.
New rulers are lords on Olympus:

New rulings from Zeus who lawlessly lords it,
The mighty of old reducing to nothing.

PROMETHEUS

I wish he had hurled me deep into Hades
Under the earth, receiver of corpses—
   Bottomless Tartarus—
Shackled unloosably, ruthlessly fastened
  Where neither a god nor another
  Could gloat his gaze on my torture.
But here I am, wretched wind-beaten plaything
  To gladden the heart of my haters.

CHORUS
Strophe 2

  Who of the gods is so brutally hearted
  That a crisis like this can proffer him pleasure?
No one but Zeus, who in anger and obstinate
                              rancor
    Oppresses the race of Ouranus
     And will not desist
     Till either he gluts
His absolute heart on it or, by some cunning,
                             another
    Seize his impregnable empire.

PROMETHEUS

  Yes, in the future the Prince of Immortals
    Shall fearfully need me
(Me in those shackles I shamefully suffered)
To discover to him the surprise and the plot
Which strips him of scepter and all his glory.

But never from *me* by honey-tongued talking,
No never from me cowering before him
  Shall the secret be opened,
Until he release me from agony bounded,
  Willing to pay me the wage
    Of this terrible outrage.

CHORUS
Antistrophe 2

O you are bold and bate not a jot
Of the bite of your torments: too free with
                                your tongue.
There strikes at my soul a fear which is shriek-
                                ing—
  A fright for your fortunes.
Where if at all and whither the haven
    You steer me to see
    The end of your beating?
For Cronus's son is hard in his hate
  With a heart that nothing can meeken.

*Epode**

One other only, one before,
Overwhelmed in the pain of adamant-
    ine bonds, the Titan god, I saw:
Atlas, preeminent in strength,
Groaning beneath the firmament
With all of heaven on his back.

PROMETHEUS

I know very well that Zeus is harsh,
Hugging his justice to himself;
* See note on page 45.

Nevertheless a day will come
When my promise shall hit him and leave him
   Sobered in wish.
Gentling down his intractable dudgeon
  He will rush to my side in affection,
  Quick to the quick to receive him.

CHORUS

Tell the tale; unveil it all.
Why did Zeus arrest you—on what charge—
To visit you with such a bitter outrage?
Explain it all to us; unless it hurts to tell.

PROMETHEUS

Even to talk of it is full of pain,
And painful to keep still. . . .
My case is hopeless every way.
  From that first moment rancor entered heaven
And discord broke among the deities—
Some wanting Cronus ousted from his throne
And Zeus put in as king,
Some wanting the reverse:
To keep Zeus out from ever governing;
Then it was that *I* tried to give them good advice
But found them hopeless to convince—
Those Titans, children of Heaven and Earth
Who, disdaining in their rugged souls my con-
                summate
Designs, assumed it was an easy thing
For force to take the mastery of Fate.[2]

[2] Elizabeth Barrett Browning's apt rendering of the line.

After the Fall of the Titans Zeus wanted the race of mortal man to be destroyed.

CHORUS

Tell the tale; unveil it all.

More than once my mother, Themis—Earth—
(She of many names but one in form)
Forewarned me of the shape of things to come:
How that not by major force or brawn
But only by sheer brain the master race would win.
Yet when I spelled this out in words to them
They would not deign even to peer
Into the truth. Whereat I thought it best,
Among the courses that were any use,
To take my mother and secede to Zeus—
A willing and a welcome volunteer.
    So, mine were the plans which made
The black abysmal Tartarus
Heap upon and hide
Age-begotten Cronus and his hosting side.
Which favor—just to "make amends"—
This despot of the gods
Pays me back in bitter pangs. . . .
Ah! Kingship wears a cancer at the heart:
A disbelief of friends.
    But as to your question, why he tortures me,
This I shall make plain.
    As soon as he was seated on his father's throne,
He apportions on the instant to each single deity
His proper perquisites and power;
Poor wretched human beings, however,
He quite left out
And thought instead to wipe away the lot
And plant a race of newer.
    No one took a stand on this but me.
I had the courage—I,
To halt men in their walk to death and to ex-
                                    tinction.
For this am I hooped in torture and abuse:
Agonies to suffer, miserable to see.

I who singled out some mercy for mankind,
Not deemed worth the same myself
But subject to this exercise so raw and so unkind:
A sight to shame the name of Zeus.

CHORUS

Heart of iron, hacked from rock,
Is any man, Prometheus, not touched to pity by
                                    your plight.
Better never to have seen it; but the sight—
Deep to my very core—makes me ache.

PROMETHEUS

I am indeed a piteous thing for friends to see.

CHORUS

But did you not sin still more grievously?

PROMETHEUS

Human beings I saved from foresight of their
                                    fate.

CHORUS

For that disease what philter did you find?

PROMETHEUS

Blind hopes I lodged within their breasts.

CHORUS

A mighty boon, that was, given to mankind.

PROMETHEUS

I also gave them fire.

CHORUS

Fire with its eye of flame!
Do the day-beings have that now?

PROMETHEUS

Yes, and shall learn a thousand arts from it.

CHORUS

These, then, are the charges on which Zeus——

PROMETHEUS

Tortures me and gives me no respite.

CHORUS

But is there never any limit set?

PROMETHEUS

Oh, none at all—except what he sees fit.

CHORUS

What *he* sees fit! What hope of that
When don't you see you sinned?—
A sin no joy to hear and only pain to tell.
But let's leave that; you must begin
A search for some release.

PROMETHEUS

How easy for the man whose foot is free from ill
To encourage and advise the one that's down!
I knew it well, and willingly
By my own free will I sinned—I'll not say "no."
In helping men I helped myself to pain;
But . . . to punishment like this . . . I never
                                                    thought:
To wasting away amongst these windy rocks . . .
                                            Ah no!
So keep your sympathy for what I suffer now.
Come down to earth and hear of what's to come
And then you'll know it end to end.
    Let yourselves—oh, let yourselves—share pain
With one who mourns today;
For suffering walks the world—alas the same—
And sits besides us all in turn.
        [*The* CHORUS *of nymphs leaves the chariot*
        and dances delicately round PROMETHEUS
                                    while singing]

CHORUS

Your prayer, Prometheus, we are ready
        Precisely to hear.
So, footing it neatly, stepping away from
My speeding seat in the spotless air—
The pathway of birds—I alight on the craggy
    Ground where I long to hear
    Your story of despair.
        [OCEAN—OCEANUS—*enters mounted*
                    on a monstrous bird]

OCEANUS

*And never let it be said that a stauncher
Friend was yours than Oceanus.*

OCEAN

Here I am finally after a tedious
Passage towards you, arriving, Prometheus,
Driving this monster bird of mine
All by my will power and no bridle.
Of course I am very distressed by the turn
Of your fortunes. The fact that we are related
        I find so affecting.
But even apart from family connections
There is no one I cherish more than you.
This you shall certainly know: for it never
Is in me to mouth away empty confections.
Come, give me a sign of how I can help you;
And never let it be said that a stauncher
Friend was yours than Oceanus.

PROMETHEUS

So! . . . What is this I see? Have *you* come too
To gape at my distress? What gave you spleen
To leave the stream named after you,
        The rocky-ceilinged caves self-hewn
And hurry to this mother land of iron?
Or are you here to gaze and grieve with me
        So full of wounds,
        Sad spectacle to see:
This friend of Zeus, who helped him to his sov-
                                    ereignty,
        Bent low in pain,
        And by the same?

OCEAN

Yes, Prometheus, I see,
And I would urge on you—

Nimble-witted though you are—
A better point of view:
Know yourself and learn new ways,
So match a king of gods who's new.
For if you fling such sharp and flinty words
                                         about,
Zeus—even from his far high throne—may hear;
Then these present miseries, this rout,
Will look like childish playing.
    Ah! Poor baited soul,
Put off this bitterness that's yours
And try to find some palliative to pains.
Even if you think I'm talking platitudes, it's true:
Your stricken state, Prometheus, is certainly the
                                              fruit
Of a much too saucy tongue; yet *still*
You won't be humble or submit to troubles: you
Want to pile them up, fresh ones on the old.
    Take me for your tutor,
Don't kick against the goad;
Seeing that a ruthless autocrat,
Irresponsible, has rule.
    Now I go, but I shall do my best
To disenthrall you from these pangs.
Be still and give your reckless speech a rest;
For don't you know with all your master man-
    agement:
A tongue too fresh gets whipped in chastise-
                                           ment?

PROMETHEUS

Oh, I am glad you manage to keep clear
    Of censure, though you dare
    Come to join me here.

Forget it now and don't concern yourself.
Do what you will you won't win *him*.
Be careful not to hurt yourself.

OCEAN

So good at dealing out advice
To all your neighbors but yourself.
Fact not fancy is the proof.
You cannot try to hold me back;
For this I know, I know that Zeus
Will give me this: to let you loose.

PROMETHEUS

For *that* I thank you and shall never cease;
Your devotion is complete. . . . Do not exert your-
                                                self:
An empty exercise—it is no use . . .
If exercise is what you want.
Hush yourself and keep away.
I'm not one when fortune strikes
To want the whole world stricken too.
No, when even my brother Atlas' plight
Weighs me down: standing westwards there
With heaven and earth pillared on his shoulders—
No easy load to bear.
    And pity moved me when I saw
That earth-sprung being,
Haunter of Cilician caves,
The hundred-headed freak, the terrifying
Great bounding Typhon, violently erased.
    He stood against the universal gods,
Hissing slaughter from his horrid jaws
And lancing grisly pangs of light from out his eyes,

[handwritten margin note: ✻ In the battle of the titans Atlas played a role against zeus and was forced to hold up the heavens with his hands.]

To obliterate if possible the sovereignty of Zeus.
    But Zeus's sleepless shaft came at him:
Bolted thunder with its breath of fire
Which struck him from his braggart eminence in
                                        terror—
Blighted to the heart, crumbled to a cinder,
His strength ripped out by the lightning blast.
    Now, a paralyzed and sprawling trunk,
He lies along the narrows of the sea,
Rammed beneath the roots of Aetna;
Whilst high upon the peaks Hephaestus sits
Hammering the molten ore.
    From there one day rivers of fire
Shall burst with raging jaws
To feast upon the level fields of fruitful Sicily.
Such shall be the boiling fury
Typhon spurts in seething jets,
Unapproachable, with squalls of flame;
Charred out though he be
By Zeus's blazing bolts.
    You, however, are no novice
And need no lessoning from me.
I shall drain my own disaster to the dregs
And wait such time as Zeus's anger goes.

OCEAN

    Surely you knew that words, Prometheus,
are doctors of a temper in disease?

PROMETHEUS

    Only if they soothe the heart in season;
not press with violent hands a swollen ire.

OCEAN

But what damage do you see
if daring joins devotion? Tell me that.

PROMETHEUS

Waste of effort and a vain naïveté.

OCEAN

Leave me, then, to sicken with that sickness.
It pays the most intelligent, most to seem a fool.

PROMETHEUS

My own mistake, it seems, exactly.

OCEAN

Your observation clearly sends me packing.

PROMETHEUS

Only to stop my own distress from winning hate
for *you.*

OCEAN

Hate from that new sitter on the seat of all-
control?

PROMETHEUS

Yes, him: beware of anger stirred in *him.*

OCEAN

Prometheus, *your* disaster is my pedagogue.

PROMETHEUS

Then go, beware, and keep it in your mind.

OCEAN

Even as I go you chase me with farewell:
Look, my four-footed bird with beating wings
Fans the wide savannas of the air—
Blithe to be home and bend his knees inside his stall.

[*Exit* OCEAN]

CHORUS
Strophe 1

I weep for your perishing fortunes,
Prometheus, in floods from the fountains
Of tears on my cheeks from my eyes—
      In watery coursing.
For Zeus on his own is inventing
Abominable laws and is shaking
His arrogant spear in the faces
Of the gods of the days gone before.

Antistrophe 1

Now is the land and echo
Of wailing and loud lamentation
For greatness and glory gone:
The times of your brothers and graces.
All nations of mortals in holy

Asia are mourning and sharing
The sufferings you are bearing
Beyond all measure of grieving.

Strophe 2

And the virgins who dwell in fair Colchis,
Maidens fearless in fight;
The Scythian hordes, the retainers
Of the rim of the world round the lake
Of Maeotis most remote;

Antistrophe 2

And the flower of Arabia in arms,
Garrisoned high on the heights
Sublime of the Caucasus near—
That bellicose host with their yell
Thundering at point of the spear;

Epode [8]

And the boom of the waves as they fall
    In murmuring deeps,
And the cloisters of Hades that roll
    Dark thunder in earth,
And the wells of the streams from their pure
    Sources bewail
    In moan for your pain.

[8] Another epode, which immediately precedes this one in
the Greek text (lines 425–430 in the Loeb Classics edition) is
possibly spurious and certainly misplaced. Its position here—
by all the internal evidence of sense, context and meter—is to
my mind ridiculous and I have put it instead immediately after
Antistrophe 2 on page 33).

PROMETHEUS

I am silent—
But not from pride,
Do not think it, nor from self-conceit
It is, that contemplation and the vision eat
My heart out: of myself so mauled.
Yet, who but *I* distributed at all
To these new gods their different gifts complete?
So I am silent, or else should tell
Of things you know. . . . But let me speak
Of the miseries of men, helpless children till
I gave them sense and ways to think. . . .
Though I do not mention man through any blame
But only to unfold the love with which I gave.
   Those first had eyes to see, but never saw;
Ears for hearing, but they never heard.
Like huddled shapes in dreams, they used to drag
Their long lives through, confusing all:
Knew no brick-built homes to front the sun,
No woodwork; but beneath the soil
They lived like tiny ants recessed in sunless holes;
No measured sign for winter, flowery spring,
Nor summer full of fruit;
Without a clue they practiced everything,
Until I showed the stars to them,
Their rising and their set—
So difficult to calculate.
   And numbers, too, I found them,
The key to sciences;
And letters in their synthesis—
Secret of all memory, sweet mother of the arts.
   I was the first to break beasts to the yoke
And bring them to the collar and the saddle,
So make them take on mankind's heaviest work.

I fixed the horse submissively to carriages:
Golden symbol of luxury and state.
And I was the one—none other—to invent
The seaman's ocean-roaming chariots with linen
wings. . . .
I, poor fool, who found for men these things
And now myself bereft of *one* expedient
To lessen this my sad predicament.

CHORUS

Unsuitable, unkind predicament!
Blank of mind and wandering—
Like some clumsy doctor fallen ill
Hopelessly and wondering
What to give himself to heal.

PROMETHEUS

Ah! Listen to the rest; be more amazed
At all the arts I found, and all the ways.
The greatest: that when a man fell ill
There was no remedy at all,
No diet, liniment or draught. So men decayed
To skeletons for lack of drugs,
Until I showed them how to mix emollient recipes,
So keep away from all disease.
And many the modes of mantic art I classified:
I first distinguished dreams that must come true.
I unraveled them the doubtful voices and the cue
To wayside auguries;
Analyzed the flight of claw-foot birds of prey—
Those essentially auspicious and the sinister—
Their varieties of life and mutual feuds,
Their loves and their consortings;

The sleekness of their entrails too:
The tinge the gall must have to please the gods.
And the shot-silk luster of their liver-lobes;
And the thigh bones wrapped in fat,
And the long chine burned—the source
Whereby I led men to an occult art.
Then I cleared their vision—once obscure—
To the red-eyed vision in the fire.
  So much for these.
Now come to human blessings hidden in the earth:
Brass, iron, silver, gold . . .
Who claims he uncovered these before me?
Oh, none—I know for sure—
Unless he wants to babble idly.
The whole truth in a sentence, if you want it short,
Is: Every art to man Prometheus brought.

CHORUS

But now you must not succor men beyond all
                                        merit,
    Careless of your own sad state.
For still I think that from these claims you shall be
                                        loosed,
    Not weaker by one whit than Zeus.

PROMETHEUS

No, not thus shall Moira, Queen of the Fates, end
                                        this.
    Ten thousand pangs and agonies must bend me
Before I shall have shaken off these chains which
                                        pen me.
    Necessity has twice the strength of artifice.

CHORUS

Who then is controller of Necessity?

PROMETHEUS

Three-personed Fate and the unforgetting
Furies.

CHORUS

Surely Zeus is not less strong than they?

PROMETHEUS

He is: at least he cannot dodge what is ordained.

CHORUS

Ordained? . . . for Zeus, is surely everlasting
sway?

PROMETHEUS

Too early still for you to know. You must not
pry.

CHORUS

Some holy secret, is it? A mystery you hide?

PROMETHEUS

Think of some other theme; the time is far from
ripe

To talk of this. Ah no! It must be hidden deep.
To break my unkind shameful fetters and escape,
   This precisely is the secret I must keep.

CHORUS

Strophe 1

   Never may Zeus who fosters
      The world in his might,
   Collide in his will against mine.
Never may *1* be remiss in offering the gods
   Worship of banquets—oxen slain—
By the runneling stream of Ocean, my father.
      Never by word may I trespass.
      This mind be mine forever
         And never grow faint.

Antistrophe 1

   Oh, it is sweeter to linger
      Long through a life
   Bright with confident hopes:
The heart made fatter with glad good cheer.
   But you, yes *you*, make me shudder:
Racked by tortures none can number,
   Refusing to bow before Zeus,
Deliberately honoring man to excess—
      O, Prometheus!

Strophe 2

Now do you see, my friend, the disgrace of your
                                          graces?

IO

What land? What race? What vision before me?

Where is there help—hurry to tell me?
Where any stay in beings of a day? Did you see
The pitiful strength of their weakness?
A dream in which men go—blind generation of
shackled;
With never a breakthrough by mortals
Of Zeus's riveted system.

Antistrophe 2

This is the lesson I learned when I gazed on the
downfall
Of your fortunes in ruins, Prometheus.
How different now—it steals on my heart—to the
tune,
The epithalamion hymning,
I sang by your bath and your bridal bed at your
wedding,
When you courted with many a love-gift
My sister, Hesione, and led her as wife to her
bed-ing.

[*Enter* IO, *distraught, and wearing horns to
symbolize her metamorphosis into a heifer*]

IO

What land? What race? What vision before me?
What rock-trammeled creature lies open
To this wintery beating?
What sin and what penance for such dissolution?
Show me a sign
Of where on earth, forlorn, I have wandered?
Aha! Aha! Poor me!
Again the gadfly stings me, miserable roamer:

Ghost of the earth-born Argus. . . . Keep him away,
   Sweet Earth—that million-eyed cowman
     Who fills me with fear . . .
His crazed-cunning eyes, marching onward.
Even in death no grave to muffle him.
But, slipping the shades, still he hounds me
   Fretted and famished
    Along the sands of the sea.

Strophe 1

And the waxen reed in the drone of its pipe
Humming a burden heavy with sleep. . . .
Where, O where, in my wandering course
   Now am I driving?
What was the sin—what?—Cronus's son,
You caught me committing so to enmesh me
   In muzzles of pain? Oh!
   Striking a timorous maiden
   To this frenzy of sting-started fright.
Consume me with fire or cover the earth on me,
Or feed me as food to the sea-deep beasts,
   But do not disdain me,
   My lord, as I plead.
Much am I schooled in many meanderings
But never a lesson on how to escape
   The sting of my troubles.
Can you hear the bleat of this ox-horned maiden?

PROMETHEUS

   How can I fail to hear
   The gadfly-driven daughter
   Of Inachus—enkindler
   Of the heart of Zeus,

Who in never-ending chase
Through Hera's hate is whipped along?

IO

Antistrophe 1

But how do you utter the name of my father?
Tell me, the woebegone, who can you be
That somehow—unhappy one—unhappy
        maiden—
 You rightly address me,
Naming the god-sent disease which devours me,
Driving me mad with the fret of its stinging? . . .
 Leaping up—aah!—
 Lashed onward by hunger and here
An agonized victim of Hera's revenge.
Who among all the unhappy ones *is* there,
Oh, oh, quite so unhappy
 As me in my pains?
 Define to me clearly
Whatever I still have to suffer:
What salve, what remedy, what for my malady *is*
         there?
 Tell if you know it,
 O speak it, declare it
To the wretched wandering damsel.

PROMETHEUS

I shall tell you clearly all you want to apprehend,
Not wrapping up in riddles but in simple speech
We rightly use to open lips to friends:
He whom you see is
Fire-giver to the race—Prometheus.

IO

Oh, you burst on men a universal benefit!
My poor Prometheus, what right have you to suffer
so?

PROMETHEUS

I have just now given over grieving for my pains.

IO

But won't you grant me my request?

PROMETHEUS

Say which request? From me you can learn the
lot.

IO

Show me, then, who locked you in this cleft?

PROMETHEUS

The plan was Zeus's: the hand Hephaestus's.

IO

In punishment for what particular crime?

PROMETHEUS

I have said sufficient and made it clear.

IO

Then add to it the revelation of my roaming's
end.
What term is set for the forlorn wanderer?

PROMETHEUS

Better for you not to know than know.

IO

You must not hide from me what *I* must suffer.

PROMETHEUS

It isn't that I grudge you such a favor.

IO

What makes you, then, withhold from speaking
out?

PROMETHEUS

Not reluctance—no—but not to crush your
heart.

IO

Do not be kinder to myself than I.

PROMETHEUS

Since you are so keen, I'll speak. So hear.

CHORUS

No, not yet, but please us with a share as well.
First we beg the story of this maiden's malady,
> So, let her with her own lips tell
> Her crowded fate; then, learn from *you*
> What wrestling is in sequel still.

PROMETHEUS

Io, the choice is yours; be kind to them in this—
Especially as they are your father's sisters.
To weep and wail one's lot
And win the tribute of a tear
Is well worth while
From those who hear.

IO

I know no way of not consenting, Nymphs.
You shall be told—and clearly—all you ask;
Though I blush to speak of the curse in the storm,
Goddess-sent, which swooped
To cancel out my form—
And I forlorn.

For always round my maiden chamber went
Those thronging visions of the night,
Entreating me in syllables that smoothly pressed:
> "O darling greatly blessed,
> Why stay a virgin still
> When in your compass lies
> A matching in the skies?
Zeus is wounded with desire for you
And languishes to join his love with you.

The bed of Zeus, my child, you must not spurn,
  But go to Lerna's knee-deep meadows
  Where your father's cattle browse
And quench in Zeus's eye the want that burns."

  Night after night, besieged by suchlike dreams,
Distressed, I dared at last to tell my father; dreams
Were haunting me; and he
To the fanes of Pytho and to Dodona
Sent many a messenger to learn
What act or spoken formula could please
The gods. But they came back with messages
Of oracles ambiguous and blind and dark to tell,
Until at last there came to Inachus
A clear response: the mandate that enjoined
That he should put me from my home and land
To wander to the confines of the world;
And, would he not,
A thunderbolt redhot
Would fall from Zeus,
Eradicating all his race.
  By these Apollo's oracles well subdued,
He drove me out and shut me from my home:
Unwilling the unwilled, but forced by Zeus's bit.
And all at once my shape and soul were warped;
Horned as you see me and goaded by the stinging
                                 fly
I plunged with maniac bolting to the happy stream
Of Cerchnea and Lerna's spring.
But the cowherd, Argus, with barbaric savaging
Pressed upon me, ever peering
With his crowded eyes and leering . . .
Until a sudden fate snatched life from him,
Leaving me to smart with the gadfly's sting,
Divinely lashed from land to land.

Such is my past. You've heard.
And if you know what toils remain, then tell.
Let no warm pity speak me lies.
The worst disease of all, I say,
Is fabricated speeches and disguise.

CHORUS

Oh! Oh! Away the thought!
Never did I—could I—think
A shock of words should so assault.
This vision hurts; it hits the sight:
Damage, degradation, dread
Smites my soul with double edge.
Life, O life! Unhappy lot
Which falls—shudder—on Io's head.

PROMETHEUS

You wail too soon: you are too full of fear.
Wait for the rest. Ah, wait and you shall hear!

CHORUS

Tell us. Speak it out. There's comfort for the sick
To know before how much remains to ache.

PROMETHEUS

Your former wish you won from me with ease:
The wish to learn from her her own ordeal.
Now hear the rest: the struggle that this girl,
And she so young, Hera will compel to face.
    Io, seed of Inachus, take my words to heart
And con the limits of your wanderers' chart.

First from this spot toward the rising sun
Turn and traverse the uncultured plains
Until you reach the nomad Scythians
Who live high up in wattled huts on wains,
Wheeled, and fortified with twanging long-shot
bows.

Keep clear of them and on
Through their land along
The roaring echoes of the rocky shore.
On your left there dwell the Chalybes—
Metalworkers—and of them beware,
For they are quite untamed
And not for strangers to come near.
    You come next to the river called Hybristes,
"Frisky," rightly named.
Attempt no ford, for it is hard to breach,
Until you reach Mount Caucasus, the loftiest pitch
Of ranges, from whose brow this river's leap
Is strength outpoured. And there you climb and
cross

Its horns that tip the stars,
And tread a southward path
Which leads you to the man-misliking Amazons,
Who one day shall settle at Themiscyra
Upon the river Thermodon,
Where Salmydessus gnashes at the sea
And like a stepdame cruelly
Welcomes ships and sailors in.
    The Amazons will put you on your way most
willingly;
And just at the narrow portals of a firth
You shall reach the isthmus called Cimmerian.
Put this behind you with undaunted heart
And swim Maeotis Strait:
A crossing afterwards made legendary for man

And named from you "the Bosporus." [4]
And so you pass from Europe's plain to Asia's
                                    continent.
   O, Nymphs—you see—the king of gods
Makes no exceptions to his ruthlessness at all:
A god who hankers for a mortal girl
Yet puts on her this roaming spell.
   Ah, fair child,
What bitter suitor have you wooed
When all you've heard
You would not even think the prelude!

IO

Misery! O misery!

PROMETHEUS

What! Crying out and groaning *now?*
How will you take what's still to come?

CHORUS

No: don't say there's suffering still to come!

PROMETHEUS

A sea of it: breaking headlong in a storm.

IO

What use my life then? And why did I not fling
Myself from off this precipice of stone?

[4] Ox-ford.

IO

What use my life then?

So dash my pangs to freedom on the plain.
Better, surely, once to die than suffer day by day!

PROMETHEUS

Ah! It would be difficult for you to bear my own
                                              ordeal,
To whom all death is disallowed:
Death who frees from pain.
Now for me there is no limit set to trouble
Till Zeus himself from kingship fail.

IO

What! Shall Zeus's kingdom ever fail?

PROMETHEUS

An event, I think, that you would like to see.

IO

Why not, indeed, when from Zeus precisely I
                                              travail?

PROMETHEUS

These things, you may be sure, are so.

IO

Through whom shall his imperial sceptership be
                                              snatched?

PROMETHEUS

Through his own self-will and vanity.

IO

In what way? Tell it if no harm.

PROMETHEUS

He shall make a match one day to cause him woe.

IO

Heavenly or human, which? Speak if you can
say.

PROMETHEUS

Why ask which? It may not be described.

IO

Shall it be his bride that makes him lose his
throne?

PROMETHEUS

Exactly that. She bears a son much stronger than
the sire.

IO

With no way out for him from such a snare?

PROMETHEUS

If I am not unloosed from fetters—never.

IO

And who, against the will of Zeus, shall be
untier?

PROMETHEUS

One of your own descendants it must be.

IO

What! A child of mine release you from your
misery?

PROMETHEUS

Yes, in thirteen generations; spell out ten and
three.

IO

Now your divination's past my guessing.

PROMETHEUS

Save your troubles—cease your searching.

IO

You must not proffer me a favor then refuse it.

PROMETHEUS

I give you choice of one of two disclosures.

IO

One of two? Produce them. Let me choose it.

PROMETHEUS

I do. Then choose. I make clear to you
Either what you must still go through
Or who shall let me loose.

CHORUS

Of these favors, give *her* one
And bless *me* with the other, please.
To her unfold her roamings still to come;
To me your looser. This *I* choose.

PROMETHEUS

Since you are so bent on it I'll not oppose
Expounding to you every word you crave.
First, Io, to you I'll tell your mazy wanderings.
Engrave them in your heart on tablets for re-
                                    membering.
When you have crossed the stream
(The refluent fringe between two continents)
Pick up your course where the sun-eyed morning
                                    starts
And cross the purring seas until you reach
The Gorgonean flats of Cisthene,
Where the Phorcides, those antique spinsters, live:

Three swan-shaped freaks—a single eye between
them
And a single tooth—on whom no sunbeams give.
Nor ever the moon-night ray.
  Next to them their three-winged sisters are:
The man-detested Gorgons with their serpent-
twisted hair,
Whom no human being can look upon and live....
Of *such* the peril I bid you to beware.
Yes, and another horrid sight—take heed!—
Those hawk-mouthed hounds of Zeus who have
no bark:
The Griffins—guard against them;
And the one-eyed horde
Of Arimaspians on their horses, who
Live along the banks of Pluto's gold-washed flood.
Do not go near.
  Next you reach the faraway land of a dark
Race inhabiting the fountains of the sun.
The river Ethiops is there.
Wend along its banks until you come
To the cataract from where
Out of the Bibline hills, the Nile
Issues forth his worshipful sweet stream.
This will lead you to the thrice-spliced delta land,
Nilotis, where at last—poor Io!—
You and your descendants are ordained
To found your distant colony.
  If any of this is indistinct, not easy to determine,
Ask me again and learn it thoroughly.
More leisure than I wish is mine.

CHORUS

But if there *is* a thing still left
For you to say or to explain

Of her most dreary flight—then say it out.
If, however, you have uttered everything
Then grant us in our turn
That grace we asked, if you recall. . . .

PROMETHEUS

She has been told her journey to the end,
But just to show that what she's heard is no vain
tale
I shall describe what she endured before she
came—
The best proof I can give of what I say,
Though leaving out the most, the vast array
Of incident, and pushing to the latest point
Of you—astray.
You had come, then, to the basin of Molossia,
Cupped by high-backed Dodona,
Where the oracular fane of Zeus Diviner
Has its miracle of talking oaks
Which in utter clarity and unperplexed
Saluted you as wife of Zeus, glorious and next
(Is that slightly sweet to you?) . . .
Until you lunged in madness, gadfly-driven,
Along the side-paths of the sea,
Coming to the mighty gulf of Rhea
Which tossed you back on your itinerary
And made that dent from the deep—believe it so—
Called the Ionian Sea,
In memory amongst men of where you went.
Let this be proof to you that my intelligence
Somewhat sees beyond the things in evidence.
The rest I shall recount to you and them together,
Picking up the track of my former sense.
There is a town, Canopus, on the very lip and
border

Of the Nile's mouth, built upon its silt-bar:
There at last shall Zeus restore your mind
By the mere touch and caress of his unalarming
hand.
And, named after Zeus's own engendering act,
Epaphus or "Touch-born" shall be born to you:
A son who garners in the fruit
Of all that broad and Nile-ly watered land.
   Then, fifth in line from him, a female race
Shall come again to Argos (well against their
wills):
Fifty virgins in full flight
From nuptials with their cousins who,
Passion-fierce—
Like falcons after ringdoves—sue
A mating unpursuable, unchaste,
Till God between their bodies slips his curse[5]
And Greece receives at dead of night
By the dastard war of women's strokes
Bridegrooms' bodies: each her man
Stripped of life; the two-edged sword
Steeped in the victims' throats . . .
(Oh, come such a love upon my foes!)
   But one of the girls with tender longing
Keeps from killing the swain beside her;
All her resolution blunted
Into choosing
The lesser of two woes:
Name of coward rather than of killer.
She in Argos shall give birth to a kingly line. . . .
But that would take a treatise to explain;
Enough to say that from her shall be born

[5] An ambiguous line in the Greek. I have taken refuge in a paraphrase and tried to combine all the possibilities in one—*and* the ambiguity.

A warrior mighty with the bow:
A man to strike these fetters off of mine.
  Such is the oracle my age-begotten mother told
Me, Themis, Titaness. . . . The manner and the
                                            means
Would need a lengthy time to tell;
Which for you to know would be no help at all.

10

        Eleleu! Eleleu!
The spasm and pain are on me again;
Ebullient frenzy stinging the brain:
    The gadfly's fireless burn.
A battering heart in my breast with fear,
  Reeling eyes which whirl as I veer
      With the blast of a maniac wind
  Away from my course; and a runaway tongue
With a syllable stream that riots and tosses
    In utter black billows of losses.

            [10 *plunges from the scene*]

                CHORUS

            Strophe 1

  Wise, very wise was the wight
First to consider and say with his tongue
  That marriage within one's degree
Was best by far, and never to meddle a match
    With either the frittering rich
    Or the pedigree-mongers of grand
    Descent—if you work with your hands.

Antistrophe 1

Never O never, make *me,*
You venerable Fates, a vision to see:
Approaching the bride-room of Zeus,
Or ever bewedded to bridegroom from heaven.
I shiver
At her maidenhood all in abuse:
Mangled and marred, poor Io, let loose
Before Hera's vagabond curse

Epode

A mating of course which is matched in degree,
I view without qualms. So, never on *me,*
Ineludible light of the love
Of the mightier gods glance down from above:
Unfightable fight, ineluctable Fate—
For what I should do, I don't see:
How escape or refuse
The intentions of Zeus?

PROMETHEUS

Zeus, indeed, with his absolute will—
He shall be humbled still:
Groomed for a marriage which hurtles him
Into oblivion from sovereignty and throne.
Then shall be consummated perfectly
The curse his father, Cronus, summoned down
Even as *he* was toppled from his ancient throne.
There's no averting such catastrophe;
None of the gods can show a way, but me.
I know it and I know the means.
So, let him sit there now so self-assured:

Trusting to his overclanging dins,
His shivered fistfuls, hurled, of snorting fire.
None of these—not one—can salvage him
From crashing into deep disgrace and groveling
ruin.
At this moment he himself
Equips against himself
A baffling antagonist terrible to fight,
Inventor of a better bolt than lightning,
Of reverberations grander than the thunder:
Smasher of Poseidon's trident—
(That sea-flail and the earth's convulser).
Wrecked by such reversal Zeus shall learn
How great the gulf between a slave and sovereign.

CHORUS

Your attack on Zeus, perhaps, is only wishes.

PROMETHEUS

Wishes, yes, but wishes that will win.

CHORUS

Then must we really look for Zeus's overthrow?

PROMETHEUS

Yes: see him saddled with far greater anguishes.

CHORUS

Don't you tremble to let such tauntings loose?

PROMETHEUS

Why should I fear, with no destiny to die?

CHORUS

But he could make your ordeal worse than this.

PROMETHEUS

I am prepared for everything. So let him try.

CHORUS

Oh, wise are the ones who bow before the
                                        Absolute!

PROMETHEUS

Bow down, adore and cringe
Before each ruler of the day.
For me your Zeus is less than nought;
So let him play at what he wants
And lord it for his little day.
His time for ruling gods is short. . . .
    But look, over there I see
Nothing less than Zeus's lackey:
This upstart despot's myrmidon
With news of course he's freshly brought.
                              [*Enter* HERMES]

HERMES

    Ah, *you* sir!
You the wise one, you the sharpest of the sharp,
You the gods' affronter, toadying to men,

Yes, you the fire-filcher—to you I speak.
The Father asks you divulge this vaunted liaison
Which makes him fall from his desmesne.
Explain it all, Prometheus:
Each item, and no mysteries—
And not a second journey on a mission, please.
Toward such sulkiness, you see, Zeus does not
grow weak.

PROMETHEUS

Oh, the pomposity, the superfine conceit
Of such a speech! It fits an errandboy
Of gods so new in youth and rule they think
They live on heights too high for grief.
From these same heights—ah!—have I not seen
Two monarchs fall? As now the third, this mo-
ment's king,
I shall see fall most shamefully and swift tomor-
row. . . .
Yes, new gods, but do you think I quail and cringe?
I leave such feelings far behind. . . . And you
can scurry
Back along the path you came.
From me you'll gather not a thing.

HERMES

So this was the brazen willfulness—yes, quite
the same—
That sent you beating to this anchorage of pain!

PROMETHEUS

I would not barter all my suffering for your
servitude:
Not I—I'll tell you plain.

HERMES

You seem to revel in your present use!

HERMES

No: servitude to stones, like these, you'd rather
                                                    claim
Than faithful heralding for Father Zeus.

PROMETHEUS

Your insolence is perfect to the pattern of abuse.

HERMES

You seem to revel in your present use!

PROMETHEUS

I revel? Then the revelers ought to be
My enemies—among them you—for me to see.

HERMES

So *I'm* to blame somehow for your catastrophe?

PROMETHEUS

Yes, for I detest—in a word—every deity
Whom I was kind to, but he unkind to *me*.

HERMES

You strike me as uncommonly insane.

PROMETHEUS

If insanity consists in hating enemies—insane.

HERMES

How insufferable you'd be if doing well!

PROMETHEUS

I am appalled!

HERMES

A word unknown to Zeus.

PROMETHEUS

Never mind! Time grows up and teaches all.

HERMES

Yet you, it seems, did not learn common sense.

PROMETHEUS

No; or I'd not be parleying with a slave.

HERMES

So: you won't tell the Father what he craves?

PROMETHEUS

I owe him a great deal, of course. It's time I gave.

HERMES

You're making fun of me as if I were a child.

HERMES TO PROMETHEUS

You come into the sun again...Ah then!

PROMETHEUS

And are you not a child, sillier than a child,
If you look to me to learn a thing?
There is no torture or device that Zeus can use
To twist me into speaking out . . .
Not until he breaks these crushing shackles loose.
So let him fling his blanching strokes of light
Or shake the world together and confound,
With his snows winged white
And mumbling ground.
None of this will make me bend and tell
The name of him by whom his kingdom fell.

HERMES

If you think this course can possibly re-
dound——

PROMETHEUS

It was all foreseen and settled long ago.

HERMES

Confront your fate, you fool! For once confront:
Resolve your sufferings into sense and bow.

PROMETHEUS

You might as well be shouting at the sea—a
billow.
Never think that any fear of Zeus' intent
Will make me womanish—uplifted hands

So feminine—to importune my greatest hate
To break these bands. I'm far from that.

HERMES

  I say too much and seem to speak in vain.
You are not moved; you do not melt
At any prayers of mine;
But like a colt being broken in
You champ the bit
And strain against the rein.
Yet what a feeble notion makes you rage:
This silly-minded mere self-will—
It does not make you strong at all.
And if my words do not persuade you, think
What a tempest, what a wave
Of threefold devastation will
Sweep over you beyond escape.
This jagged cliff the Father first will break
With thunder and his bolting fire,
To cover you embraced (but still entire)
By arms of rock. And then,
After ages of completed time,
You come into the sun again. . . . Ah then!
Zeus's flying hound, the eagle red for flesh,
With savage appetite shall climb
Unbidden down, the whole long day,
To scissor up your carcass in great strips,
Glutting on the blood-black fodder of your liver.
  Nor can you look for any respite from this stress
Until some god appear to take upon himself your
                                              work
And of his own free will go down to Hades' dark,
Deep into Tartarus' Stygian shaft.
  Think of this. It is no bluff or threat

PROMETHEUS

He shall not kill me still.

But uttered in great earnestness.
The mouth of Zeus is impotent to lie:
Every syllable he brings to pass.
Be circumspect, reflect;
And never for a moment think that stubbornness
Is better than good common sense.

CHORUS

What Hermes says seems opportune to us.
He asks you only to lay down your stubbornness,
Go seek a little thoughtfulness and good advice.
Studied sin is shame to a man who's wise.

PROMETHEUS

He cries this news to one who knows;
Yet where's disgrace when enemies
Receive from enemies their blows?
  So let the lightning fork
  And coil about my head.
  Let thunder rip the sky;
  Wild winds stampede
And wreck. A hurricane to rock
    The rooted world
    From its pedestal.
  Let sea waves slash their tide
  Across the path of stars.
  Let him fling my carcass deep
  Where the sterile eddy stirs
    Of Anangke's spell:
  He shall not kill me still.

HERMES

Such thoughts and words one thinks to hear
From raving men. Where does it fall

Short of a thing, this plea, from sheer
  Mania, or miss
  Madness on the run?
And you who sympathize
With what his ordeal is,
Move away from here
Lest the thunder's roar
Stun you out of sense.
Stun you to the core.

CHORUS

Another voice, another bidding
You must use—and more convincing.
Your proposal goes too far.
Can you ask me mean behavior?
What *he* must suffer, *I* am willing.
Traitors I have learnt to hate.
  There is no pest
  I so abominate.

HERMES

Well then, keep in mind my warning
When you're caught in your disaster;
Do not blame your fates or say
Zeus propelled you into groaning;
Not at all—but blame yourselves.
  Unsurprised, not secretly,
    And only after
    Full forewarning,
You were in the net of Atè—
  Tangled inextricably
  And through your folly.

[*Exit* HERMES]

PROMETHEUS

Now comes the act; no more the threat:
The earth is rocking.

PROMETHEUS

Now comes the act; no more the threat:
    The earth is rocking.
Thunder reverberate roaring near;
Scintillant twist of wreathing fire.
    Winds in a funnel of dust.
    Body of gales leaping up,
    Massed in separate strife.
Sky and the deep shaken together.
See: it advances clarion clear—
Hurries from Zeus to hit me with fear.
O Mother, holy Mother, the Air,
Spinning us the light we share,
    Watch how I wickedly suffer!

[*Amid a universal bombardment of thunder
and lightning,* PROMETHEUS *together with the
daughters of* OCEANUS — *the* CHORUS — *disappear*]

APPENDIXES

I SOME NOTES ON PRODUCTION

In staging Greek drama there are two opposite dangers to guard against: treating it as if it were designed for the modern proscenium theater, and treating it as if the conventions of classical dramaturgy were in themselves all that mattered.

As to the first: the modern boxlike stage, together with the entire convention whereby the audience looks into three walls of a room and is regaled with a "slice of life," is essentially wrong for Greek drama, where the scenes take place out of doors and where it is not a replica of reality that is sought but a heightening and idealization of it. Moreover, there is hardly room on the proscenium stage for keeping chorus and actors, physically and in spirit, detached from one another. The balletic movements of the chorus are ideally mimetic, commentatory and emotive. The chorus creates the esthetic front, the formal diagram, behind which the action proceeds. It must have space and position. For this reason, Greek drama needs to be staged in the round. If a producer is not blessed with the opportunity of staging in an arena, at least let him get away from the proscenium arch: bring his boards forward, even if it means removing some of the seats.

As to the second danger, the idolizing of a con-

vention: beware of treating a Greek play as if it
were a museum piece. The formalities of classical
drama are there for us to use and not slavishly
copy. I have seen productions in which the quest
for historical authenticity has been allowed to obliterate everything that made the play worth while.
Another obsession which seems to grip many a
director is overstylization. This means stilted acting, preposterous costumes, false voices. It is true
that there is a ritualistic, even a liturgical dignity
to Greek tragedy, but a valid formula must be
devised for making this flow evenly and naturally.
The fact that the characters—however different
their story and setting—are prearchaic Greeks
moving around in a heroic landscape—is of far
less importance than that they are human beings
endowed with feelings of love and hate and fear
exactly similar to the love and hate and fear of all
times—including our own. It is up to the director
to translate these feelings from *their* setting to
ours; and this he will hardly do if he exaggerates
the dignity and the distance. He should use the
conventions of the Greek theater as a means and
never an end.

From this it also follows that he should not try
to turn a Greek play into a piece of glorious art
and culture. If he succeeds in moving an audience,
the art and the culture will certainly be there; but
if he tries to put them in artificially, all that will
result is "artiness"—from which nine Greek plays
out of ten fail today: that is, from sheer pretension.
To my mind the secret of producing and directing
Greek tragedy is to play it for its humanity, its
feeling and its beauty.

The next point to bear in mind—probably the

most important of all—is that a Greek play stands
or falls by the quality of its sound: the sound of
the human voice. It is the words that count. The play
is made with *words*—noble speeches, cut-and-
thrusting dialogue, verbally moving choruses—not
with "visuals" as in the cinema and television. A
cardinal modern mistake is to expend energy on
what is seen rather than on what is heard. It is the
ear, thence the imagination, and only thence the
eye, that has to be stirred. The ancient Greeks went
to immense trouble to train the voice in the recita-
tion of epic, lyric, and dramatic poetry; schooling
it surely to the most subtle perfection of all: a manner that gives the illusion of being natural when in
fact it is highly formal.[1] If a director thinks that the
translation he is using will not bear the strain of
a full, rhythmical, and articulate delivery—then
let him scrap it. What is essentially unfaithful to
the first principle of Greek drama cannot be sal-
vaged by any histrionics on the part of director
or actor.[2]

How, then, should the poetry of Greek drama
be spoken? First, obviously, as poetry, i.e., as pat-
terned language rich in concept, tone, and rhythm:
these last summing up many of the qualities that
music has. One must believe that the words have

[1] Very much more formal and artificial than English poetry,
which does not on the whole use a separate language and
vocabulary.

[2] In this respect I cannot help thinking some directors are
too ready to adopt translations whose chief merit is their
clarity. Aeschylus and Sophocles, after all, are not Ibsen and
Chekhov, and many of their most moving passages are precisely where the words take wing and fly in the face of logic and
clarity.

been designed not simply to give information [8] but to make us begin to feel in certain directions, remembering also that the most brilliant acting in the world cannot go to the heart so quickly as music can.

An actor, therefore, should be conscious of the sonic and rhythmical structure of the lines he is speaking and create his effects within and not outside that pattern. Indeed, only *after* he has satisfied himself on the metrical requirements of the line should he proceed to *act*. Then he can even forget them, assured that the verbal music will show up underneath his acting and produce that special tension between sound and sense which is the wonder of poetry. He will use his natural voice: a voice bolder and more forceful than is used in ordinary theater, one well removed from what Peter Arnott calls "the wink-and-whisper school," and mere chattiness, but which he never allows to degenerate into bombast. He will not move about too much: movement is for the chorus, his foil. He will make a clear distinction in his mind between giving the illusion of ordinary speech and actually using it. The first aims at a heightened realism—ordinary speech made perfect—which is a very different thing from mere naturalism. It allows the words to "sing." The second reduces them to prose.

All this the actor will find within his means so long as he is convinced that the poet has done the greater part of the work already and that the feeling is already stored and garnered in the arrangement of the words themselves. For my own part, I

[8] Information, in fact, was scarcely necessary: the Greek audience already knew the story.

believe that the most telling performance in a
Greek play is the one in which the actor or actress
realizes what the words say, the way they say it,
and then delivers them line by line: [4] clearly, un-
hurriedly, rhythmically—beautifully. And this in-
cludes a certain zest: a frank delight in gesture
and display—the whole gamut of make-believe
that play-acting is.

When it comes to the chorus, far from this being
a tiresome accessory which gets in the way of action, it is the crux of all Greek drama. Certainly it
is the most challenging part of the classical conventions. A producer would be wise to have on his team
a first-class choreographer and ballet master—one
who well understands the art of mime. The chorus
forms the bridge between the actors and the spectators—between the characters and the outside
world. When handled with imagination and restraint, nothing so conduces to quicken an audience to wonder, apprehension, and tears. The
chorus picks up, follows, advises on, regrets, the
thoughts and actions expressed in the dialogue. It
relieves tension, and it also increases it: interpreting
and underlining. Its passages should be chanted or
spoken in unison and only divided up for single
voices when the text enjoins this. Usually the
chorus is on the stage throughout. It does not rest.
Even when not delivering its own parts it should
be moving and miming—which is not to say that
it must be running hither and thither making a

[4] It is important to give line endings their prosodic value,
even if only the subconscious ear detects this. In other words,
the end of a line must be "sounded." It is possible to make this
appear natural and inevitable even when sound militates
against sense—in which case the sense almost always gains an
unexpected impetus.

spectacle of itself. A great deal of its movement will be nonlocomotive, limited to eloquent use of the hands and body. The worst thing it can do is to emulate crowd scenes from the modern cinema, where kaleidoscopic chaos often seems to be the objective and everyone is up to something different. Simplicity of effect and not flamboyance should be the keynote. The chorus should deliver an impact which is powerful, sympathetic and beautiful—so expressive that one might almost say the spectators gain their impression of the direction of the play merely by watching the attitudes of the chorus.

Together with the chorus, of course, one must consider the music. Let there be plenty of it, but always as handmaid to the words—never master. There can be music, too, for entrances and exits and perhaps even—modestly—behind parts of the dialogue. Instrumentation, however, should be kept simple and never allowed to slow up the pace. Greek drama was played with dispatch. It is we "culture-mongers" who tend to slow it down and make it boring. As to the instruments, use whatever is needed, though compositions that call for the violin are almost certainly too romantic. The Greeks themselves, for dramatic accompaniment, employed the flute (double and single), the trumpet, the kettledrum, the syrinx (Panpipes), cymbals, and also castanets and maracas.

As to the music, I have used the most unlikely composers with telling effect: Moon Dog from the streets of New York, with all his weird combinations of percussion and flute, for the *Antigone;* Edgard Varèse, with his dissonances and climaxes of ultramodern noise, for *Oedipus the King.* The music that will support and enhance Greek drama is varied indeed. Peter Arnott in his admirable book on the Greek theater suggests using modern Greek folk tunes, or even something nearer home. He says he harnessed, with happy results, Welsh folk music to a production of Euripides' *Cyclops.* By their fruits you shall know them: when the music begins to give a new dimension to the words, blends with the mood, expands and stresses the emotions—then you will know you are not wrong.

Scenery and settings should be of the simplest, though they can be grand: symbolic and suggestive rather than realistic. It is good to give the stage as many acting levels as possible: certainly one for the chorus and one for the actors; which they can of course reverse. Steps, terraces, platforms are all useful. There should be three entrances. Gods and goddesses were made to appear from the sky with the help of the famous "machine" or could be rolled out on a dais called the "ekkyklema." The simple device of throwing open inner doors, or drawing a curtain, to reveal something momentous can also be very effective.

Costumes should not be as drab as they are often made to be. The element of spectacle in Greek plays was, and ought to be, considerable. Aeschylus taxed his imagination to the utmost to invent beautiful costumes for his actors. They were so successful, legend has it, that the priests copied them for their vestments. Here certainly was style, ornament, and plenty of color.

Whether actors nowadays should use masks or not is a question that should be settled on its particular merits. In our smaller, more intimate theaters, where the cast of the features can be seen

by everyone, masks might prove merely distract-
ing. Moreover, there is always the danger that the
actor of today, once behind a mask, will behave
like a creature from another planet. His voice
booms and whispers; he prances about; he turns
into a monolith or scythes the air like a blindfold.
On the other hand, there can be no doubt that
where style is used as a means to an end and not
an end in itself, cleverly stylized masks can catch
the predominant mood of a character and hammer
it into our sensibility at every turn. An effective
alternative to the full mask (which can hamper an
actor's diction) is heavily stylized make-up.

Here, to sum up, is the carefully distilled advice
of a modern classicist, translator and producer of
Greek plays—one who has seen their problem and
their beauty from a rare combination of view-
points:

A Greek tragedy should flow from beginning
to end without pause. Think in terms of dramatic
oratorio rather than of drama proper. The Greeks
used dramatic pauses sparingly and only to se-
cure a special effect, like a few bars' rest in a
symphony. For the most part characters entered
during speeches, not in pauses between them;
even long processional entrances were covered
by dialogue. Intervals are unnecessary when there
is no scene-changing to be done. They are fatal
to dramatic continuity, and it is not asking too
much of an audience to expect them to sit through
one tragedy without a break. Colour, speed
and movement—let these be your guiding principles.[5]

[5] Peter D. Arnott, *An Introduction to the Greek Theatre,*
London: Macmillan & Co., Ltd., 1961.

Prometheus Bound has very little dramatic action in it, even of reportage. My final advice is to play it with a certain grand simplicity, using a musical score which combines majesty with hints of tenderness—perhaps something with a touch of Elgar's *Dream of Gerontius* about it. The manner should suggest some lofty elemental tale which is hallowed, primitive, timeless, and of mysterious importance.

II   E N D - S Y L L A B L E   D O V E T A I L I N G

Two typical passages of line endings in the *Prometheus*:

1

μή τοι χλιδῇ δοκεῖτε μηδ' αὐθαδίᾳ
mē toi chlidē dokeite mēd' authad ia⟩   *1.436*
σιγᾶν με· συννοίᾳ δὲ δάπτομαι κέαρ,
sigan me; sunnoia de daptomai k ear,
ὁρῶν ἐμαυτὸν ὧδε προυσελούμενον.
horōn emauton hōde prouseloume non.
καίτοι θεοῖσι τοῖς νέοις τούτοις γέρα
kaitoi theoisi tois neois toutois g era⟩   ⟶ ¼ *rhyme*
τίς ἄλλος ἢ 'γὼ παντελῶς διώρισεν;
tis allos ē 'go pantelōs diōris en?   ⟶ *full consonance*
ἀλλ' αὐτὰ σιγῶ· καὶ γὰρ εἰδυίαισιν ἄν   ⟶ ½ *consonance*
all' auta sigō; kai gar eiduiaisi n an
ὑμῖν λέγοιμι· τὰν βροτοῖς δὲ πήματα
humin legoimi; tan brotois de pēm ata⟩
ἀκούσαθ', ὥς σφας νηπίους ὄντας τὸ πρὶν
akousath', hōs sphas nēpious ontas to pr in
ἔννους ἔθηκα καὶ φρενῶν ἐπηβόλους.
ennous ethēka kai phrenōn epēbolous. . . .

I am sil ent⟩   ⟶ ½ *consonance*   *p. 46*
But not from pr ide,
Do not think it; nor from self-con c eit⟩
It is, that contemplation and the visio n eat⟩------------⟶ *full rhyme*
My heart out: of myself so maul ed⟩   ⟶ ½ *consonance*
Yet, who but *I* distributed a t all⟩
To these new gods their different gifts compl ete?
So I am silent, or else should t ell⟩   ⟶ *full consonance*
Of things you know. . . . But let me sp eak⟩   ⟶ *assonance*
Of the miseries of men, helpless children t ill⟩
I gave them sense and ways to th ink . . .   ⟶ ½ *consonance*

2

ἃ πρὶν μολεῖν δεῦρ' ἐκμεμόχθηκεν φράσω.
ha prin molein deup' ekmemochthēken phra [sō,]   *1.825*
τεκμήριον τοῦτ' αὐτὸ δοὺς μύθων ἐμῶν.
tekmērion tout' auto dous muthōn e [mōn] ———————▶ *assonance*
ὄχλον μὲν οὖν τὸν πλεῖστον ἐκλείψω λόγων.
ochlon men oun ton pleiston ekleipsō lo [gōn;] ———▶ *full rhyme*
πρὸς αὐτὸ δ' εἰμι τέρμα σῶν πλανημάτων.
pros auto d' eimi terma sōn planēma [tōn.]
ἐπεὶ γὰρ ἦλθες πρὸς Μολοσσὰ γάπεδα.
epei gar ēlthes pros Molossa gape (da,)
τὴν αἰπύνωτόν τ' ἀμφὶ Δωδώνην. ἵνα
tēn aipunōton t' amphi Dōdōnēn, hi (na)
μαντεῖα θᾶκός τ' ἐστὶ Θεσπρωτοῦ Διὸς
manteia thakos t' esti Thesprōtou [Dios,] - - - - - - ▶ *alliteration*
τέρας τ' ἄπιστον, αἱ προσήγοροι δρύες,
teras t' apiston, hai prosēgoroi dru [es,] - - - ▶ ½ *consonance*
ὑφ' ὧν σὺ λαμπρῶς κοὐδὲν αἰνικτηρίως
huph' hōn su lamprōs kouden ainiktē [riōs] - - - - ▶ *full rhyme*
προσηγορεύθης ἡ Διὸς κλεινὴ δάμαρ
prosēgoreuthēs hē Dios kleinē da (mar)
μέλλουσ' ἔσεσθαι· τῶνδε προσσαίνει σέ τι;
mellous' esesthai; tōnde prossainei se ti? . . .

I shall describe what she endured before she (came) —   *p.-66*
The best proof I can give of what I [say,]
Though leaving out the most, the vast ar [ray] - - - - - - ▶ *assonance*
Of incident, and pushing to the latest poi (nt)
Of you — as [tray.] ——————————▶ *full rhyme*
    You had come, then, to the basin of Mo [lossia,]   ½ *rhyme* + *triple*
Cupped by high-backed [Dodona,]   *syllable*
Where the oracular fane of Zeus [Diviner] - - - - - ▶ ½ *consonance*
Has its miracle of talking oa (ks) ——————▶ ½ *consonance*
Which in utter clarity and unperp [le (xed)] ———▶ *full rhyme*
Saluted you as wife of Zeus, glorious and [ne (xt)]
(Is that slightly sweet to you?) . . .

III   AN INFORMAL SURVEY OF THE
      GREEK THEATER

(1) What main features does a Greek play of the
fifth century B.C. share with one of today?

Both are *plays*: a set of words to be spoken by
actors which pretends to unfold certain events
as well as the thoughts and feelings of two or
more characters. Both portray (presumably) some
kind of conflict; both can be either tragic or comic
or mixed; both can be written in poetic form,
though a modern play usually is not; both can use
a chorus or equivalent chorus, though a Greek
play always does and a modern play rarely; both
can proceed by the method of myth and symbol to
state ultimate ideas through the specific actions and
thoughts of characters in a story. Finally, both—
at least we hope so—set out to be some form of
art: that is, to reconstruct in a medium which is
not life, but in a way we can understand or regret
or enjoy—and in a form that is esthetically pleas-
ing—the inner and outer aspects of our human
condition.

(2) What are some of the differences?

i) The Greek theater was very much more than
a place of entertainment. In fifth-century Athens

it was also the semiritualistic expression of the culture and religion of a whole people. The plays were presented at festivals of great civic importance, to a garlanded audience. There were seats of honor for ambassadors, and visitors came from all over Greece. Later, when theaters had sprung up in almost every town of importance in the Mediterranean, drama became detached from its community origins and surrendered to a spirit of professionalism (though the profession of actor was highly honored), but in the best period it was very much a citizen art produced for a citizen audience by citizen performers. The playwrights did not hope to earn their living by it (though later the state seems to have paid an honorarium to each of the contending poets). They wrote for love of their art and in hope of renown.

ii) The Greek theater was never a mirror of superficialities, a platform for social reform, an analysis of the burdens of the common man. It did not try to produce a naturalistic replica of life but an idealized, that is, heightened, representation of it. Consequently it needed a powerful, high-geared, and inspired art to put it over: in poetry, song, and spectacle.

iii) The subject matter of Greek drama was almost always taken from the well-known stories of the gods and the heroes; consequently the plots were known to the audience in advance. The thrill of anticipation, the gradual unfolding of inevitable disaster, took the place of suspense. Dramatic irony took the place of discovery. The Greek dramatist was free to concentrate his artistry on *how* a thing was done rather than on *what* was done. He did not have to include for the sake of information or

realism the tedious and the banal. He could leave
out a great deal and thereby intensify his emotive
power.

iv) Greek drama depicted; modern drama dis-
plays. The genius of the one was to bring a scene
to life by the power of words; of the other, by
actual vision. In a Greek play erotic passion, phys-
ical violence, murder, were described verbally,
never or rarely shown. The horror of the unseen
—but imagined—took the place of the horror (all
too easily the nausea) of the seen. In a modern
play these things are shown visually rather than
described: words tend to become secondary to
what is done and actually visualized.[1] In the art
of the cinema or television words might almost be
said to have become redundant. Greek plays, on
the contrary, consisted mainly of speeches and
songs, separated by rapid passages of alternate line
dialogue (stichomythia) made exciting by the cut
and thrust of debate. The songs were musically
accompanied, mimed and danced. The form, therefore, was by no means static, the content even less
so. Precisely because the burden of having to re-
produce a visual replica of action was avoided and
the poet was free to create an illusion of idealization of reality, words took wing, crossed the seas,
fought with armies, entered the boudoirs of queens,
delved into the motives of murderers, discovered
the aspirations of heroes. There was nothing to
limit the range and power of the Greek playwright
but his own imagination and his mastery of words.

v) Greek plays took place outside. Indoor scenes

[1] I am, of course, describing the general trend, not the in-
numerable exceptions.

were either reported or revealed to the audience through the "ekkyklema," "something rolled out" —a kind of platform which was rolled out through the skene doors—though it is not impossible that interior scenes were also shown by the doors suddenly opening.

vi) Stage scenery was of the simplest sort or non-existent, though its introduction has been ascribed to both Aeschylus and Sophocles. Tragedies were usually set before a temple or palace, comedies before a street of houses. The permanent architectural background could by the mere words and gestures of an actor become the seashore, a cave or a mountain. Besides the ekkyklema there were other stage devices, the most important of which was the "machine"—a kind of crane which could make gods appear and disappear or fly through the sky. There was no artificial lighting—though torches could be used for spectacular processional effects—and all scenes, even night, were acted in broad day. To sum up: in the greatest period of Greek drama the keynote was economy of means and absolute reliance on the imaginative artistry of the spoken word.

vii) All parts were acted by male actors, of whom—since the time of Sophocles—there was a maximum of three. By changing his mask the same actor could take on two or more parts. There, were, however, extras and supers: retinues for tragic kings and queens, soldiers, servants, and attendants.

viii) Since there was no proscenium curtain (and no need for one) plays were presented without break from start to finish—an enormous saving of cumulative dramatic power.

(3) Did the Greeks have a somewhat different idea of tragedy from us?

Here is Aristotle's famous definition of tragedy, drawn from, and formulated a hundred years after, the golden age of Greek drama: "Tragedy, then, is an imitation of an action that is serious, complete, and of a certain magnitude; in language embellished with every kind of artistic ornament, the several kinds being found in separate parts of the play; in the form of action, not of narrative;[2] through pity and fear effecting the proper purgation of these and similar emotions."[3]

(4) Would you say, then, that modern tragedy (dating it roughly from Ibsen, Strindberg, and Chekhov) is more pessimistic than Greek tragedy?

In the sense that Greek tragedy did not necessarily have to end unhappily, yes; or that even when it did so the mood and intention were to reinforce rather than to undermine man's belief in the value of living—again, yes. Curiously, however, it is we and not the Greeks who tend to believe in the perfectibility of man. Yet the tone of modern tragedy has been far more pessimistic. Many of our plays leave us with little more than a painstaking record of the slow attrition and disintegration of the human person. The manner, too, is far from sublime or encouraging. We have been tempted to doubt the validity of free will, hence of personal responsibility, hence of the hero. It follows that the grand manner is suspect too. A

[2] I.e., the story is acted, not merely told.
[3] *Poetics:* 1449b.

theater that centers precisely on the "common man," often the vicious man, dwells on insight rather than on illumination. We have produced a race of playwrights that speaks brilliantly for a generation lost and disillusioned. And yet, when all is said and done, murder, suicide, incest, adultery, war, or—if one puts it in terms of emotion —anger, revenge, despair, lust, pride, power—remain equally the raw material of Greek as of modern tragedy. It is the manner rather than the matter that has changed. And if one is tempted to think that the modern approach, with all its post-Freudian insight, gets nearer to the eternal verities and to the mind and heart of man, he has simply to put Jean Anouilh's *Antigone* next to Sophocles' for his answer. In the great tragedies of Aeschylus, Sophocles, and Euripides, the courage with which the whole human situation is challenged, and the sublimity to which it is raised by the universality of the thought and the beauty of the language, are themselves vehicles of hope, gratitude, and ennoblement.

(5) How did so noble an art arise?

This is largely a matter of guesswork and there are several rival theories. What is certain is that it grew slowly through several centuries and that it developed out of choral song. This song became the "dithyramb": a kind of mimic hymn-dance performed by fifty men dressed as satyrs and celebrating the deeds of the god Dionysus, who was the deity of luxuriant fertility, especially of the vine. In time (some scholars propose: from the beginning), the deeds of other gods and heroes also

became the material for these sagas. There came into existence a body of narrative poetry essentially
dramatic in content, though not in form. The moment one of the chorus stepped aside and began
to converse with the rest as a priest-actor, a new
art sprung from the dithyramb and drama was
born. The move is traditionally ascribed to Thespis, who thus became "the Father of Drama." One
other great step was necessary before tragedy could
develop freely: the separation of the wildly fertil-
ity-minded satyric elements from the movement
of serious drama—in other words, the invention
of the satyr play. This step is said to have been
taken by Pratinas, who wrote about 500 B.C. It
was Aeschylus, according to Aristotle, who introduced a second actor [4] and thus initiated dramatic
conflict in dialogue between two characters. He
also reduced the size of the chorus from fifty to
twelve and made it active in the drama; invented
elaborate costuming and perhaps stage scenery and
the painted mask; created new dances; and wrote
the first great Greek plays that have come down
to us. Under Aeschylus the choral lyric of early
Greek drama turned into lyric tragedy: the dramatic lyric became lyric drama.

(6) You speak as though the two forms are dis-
tinct.

They are, but under Aeschylus they were fused
into one: ". . . due partly to the historical accident in which two forms of fiction were combined:

[4] Sophocles raised the number of actors to three and the
number of the chorus to fifteen. According to Aristotle he introduced scene painting.

drama, still relatively primitive and naive, with choral lyric, now after generations of mature practice, brought to its highest point of development by Simonides and Pindar. But the direction taken by the form is due also to deliberate choice. The desire is to transcend the limitations of dramatic presentation, even before these limitations have been firmly established." [5]

(7) Do we know the names of any of the tragic poets before the coming of Aeschylus?

Yes, but not their works, or only fragments. Thespis, Pratinas, Choerilus, Phrynichus, had all made some kind of name for themselves before the coming of Aeschylus. Thespis (sixth century B.C.), by introducing an actor to play against the chorus, is regarded as the father of Greek drama. Besides bringing in dialogue he enlarged the subject matter of drama, though still apparently keeping it within the Dionysian cycle of myths. It was not till about 535 B.C. that tragedy was officially recognized by the Athenian state and given publicly sponsored contests and performances.

The most famous tragic poet before Aeschylus was Phrynicus. He won his first victory in 511 B.C. and won again in 476. He seems to have been the first to break away from stories revolving round the god Dionysus and to use Homer as an inexhaustible quarry. He introduced new measures and dances for the chorus and was styled "Master of all

[5] Professor Richmond Lattimore, Introduction to his translation of the *Oresteia. Aeschylus. Complete Works.* 2 vols. ed. by David Grene and Richmond Lattimore. Vol. 1, *Oresteia.* Chicago: University of Chicago Press, 1953.

singers," whose songs were "sweet as the honey of a bee." Phrynichus also seems to have been the first to adapt contemporary events to drama. Two of his plays dealt with historical subjects, and in 494 B.C. he portrayed on the stage the capture of Miletus, which had just fallen to the Persians.

As to Choerilus of Athens, we know that he competed against Aeschylus in 499 B.C. and was at his height in 482. He seems to have been especially gifted in satyric drama, the invention of his younger contemporary, Pratinas.

A little later in the fifth century there was Ion, the popular writer and elegant stylist; the clever and facile Agathon—the first to write a drama on a subject not connected with mythology or history, whose choruses became musical interludes and whose style is said to have been florid. There were also Neophron of Sicyon, Aristarchus of Tegea, Archaeus of Eretria. They were all prolific writers, but by the unanimous consent of antiquity there was nobody to compare with the big four: Aeschylus, Sophocles, Euripedes, and Aristophanes. The next important name is that of Menander, but that takes us into the fourth and third centuries B.C., when the greatest period of Greek drama was over.

(8) From where did the Greek dramatists of the fifth century draw their material?

Principally from the old stories of the gods and heroes as handed down by oral and written tradition in epic and lyric poetry, particularly from the *Iliad* and *Odyssey* of Homer. Homer became a kind of bible-*cum*-history of the ancient world, and a compendium of its values. Occasionally a drama was built upon contemporary history, as in *The Persians* of Aeschylus—the story of the repulse by the Greeks of the mighty army of Xerxes —but in general the Greek dramatists did not depart from their sources of epic legend. Within these limits they felt free to select, expand, reshape, and interpret, drawing from them new developments of theme, plot, and character. For example, Aeschylus, Sophocles, and Euripides all wrote plays on the Oedipus cycle, though only those of Sophocles have survived.

(9) You said that the Greek theater was much more than a place of entertainment. In what way?

It never quite lost its religious motive and impetus. Even apart from its liturgical origins— hymns and dances around the altar of Dionysus[6] —Greek drama was imbued with a powerful moral and ethical sense which sought not only to inspire but to teach. The plays of the three great tragic poets—and even of the comic playwright, Aristophanes—are profoundly theological. Man's ways with God or the gods—and vice versa—are explored throughout, side by side with the ever-important and always bewildering questions of destiny, freedom, personal responsibility, and sin, especially the sin of pretension and overweening self-assertion (*hybris*). Within such an anthropotheological framework are also presented man's ways with man: honor, justice, retribution, law,

---

[6] Which became forever afterward the pivotal point in the orchestra and was called the "thymele."

liberty, duty; and his universal emotions: love, hate, revenge, fear, pride, pity, and regret. These are the themes and emotions which pulse through the stories taken by the Greek poets from their heroic past and turned by them into dramas of surpassing power, significance, and beauty.

(10) Was the Greek theater popular?

Enormously. When the young Aeschylus first came into dramatic conflict with his celebrated contemporaries, Pratinas and Choerilus, in 499, it drew such crowds that the wooden scaffolding on which the spectators sat collapsed (which led to the Athenians building their first stone theater). But even apart from the intrinsic fascination of the plays themselves, it was the right and duty of citizens to attend.

(11) When were the chief Athenian dramatic festivals?

The three most important were held every year in midwinter and spring. They were the City Dionysia (or Great Dionysia) in March/April, the Rural Dionysia in December/January, and the Lenaea in January/February. The first of these was devoted mainly to tragedy, and the third to comedy. The City Dionysia opened with two days of processions, pageantry, hymns, and dances in honor of Dionysus. The last three days were taken up entirely with drama. The three tragic poets competing each furnished a set of three tragedies and a mock-heroic pastoral called a "satyr play." These sets of four plays, tetralogies, could either elaborate on a single theme or be a collection of plays each on a different subject. Each poet was allowed a team of three (at first two) actors and a chorus of twelve or (after Sophocles) fifteen, as well as supernumeraries. There also competed five (in wartime three) comic poets, offering a play apiece. They were allowed the same number of actors but a chorus of twenty-four. In both tragedies and comedies the poets wrote not only their plays but the music and choreography to go with them. They also directed, saw to the costumes and scenery, and, at least till the time of Sophocles, acted. Sophocles seems to have been the first to discontinue this practice, considering his voice not strong enough.

(12) Who financed these proceedings?

The city shared expenses with some wealthy member of the community who was specially selected for each playwright and known as the "choregus." The authority who governed the whole festival was the "archon," and any poet wishing to compete submitted to him his plays for reading. If the plays were accepted the poet was "granted a chorus." Then it was the choregus who paid for the training and equipping of that chorus. The state paid for the actors. The winning poet was crowned with a wreath in the presence of the multitude, a distinction that made him one of the most important members of the nation. There were prizes of wreaths also for the star actor and the choregus, who was allowed to erect a monument in honor of his victory.

(13) How many people could a theater hold?

Probably between fourteen and twenty thousand, but there seems to be a surprising divergence of opinion. One modern authority gives the seating capacity of the theater at Epidaurus as seventeen thousand, of the theater at Megalopolis as nineteen thousand, and of the theater of Dionysus at Athens as fourteen thousand. However, we do not know what extra standing capacity there may have been. Plato speaks of a play of Agathon having been witnessed by thirty thousand in the same theater of Dionysus.

(14) What kind of people went to the theater?

Every kind, including children and probably slaves.[7] It was by no means a highbrow, though it seems to have been a sensitive and lively, audience. There are plenty of stories of spectators being moved to tears or anger or made wild with anticipation. In the fourth century and afterward, when the Greek theater had reached its peak and the interest of the audience had largely shifted from the poets to the actors, ". . . both Plato and Aristotle speak of poets and actors lowering themselves to suit the depraved taste of a public dominated by the less cultivated elements in it."[8] But at least in the fifth century, the century of Aeschylus, Sophocles, and Euripides, ". . . our general conclusion must be that an audience which could follow devotedly the three great tragedians day after

[7] It must be remembered that the Athenian slave could be and often was a highly educated person.

[8] Sir Arthur Pickard-Cambridge, *The Dramatic Festivals of Athens*, to which I am indebted throughout. Oxford: The Clarendon Press; New York: Oxford University Press, 1953.

day, and could enjoy the wit of Aristophanes, must
have possessed on the whole a high degree of seri-
ousness and intelligence, and though there was
always a possibility of lower elements gaining the
upper hand for a moment, the great poets . . .
never played down to them." [9]

It should be said in passing that women of the
higher classes usually stayed away from the comedies and satyr plays. These never quite lost their
nexus with the old fertility rites and motives. They
were phallic, farcical, and frankly indecent, an out-
let for animal spirits. The costumes were grotesque
and obscenely padded. And one can guess what
gestures no doubt went with them.

(15) How could the actors be heard in such vast
theaters in the open air?

The acoustics of these theaters (as can still be
tested) were amazingly good. In the large theater
at Epidaurus, for instance, a clear but not over-
loud conversation on the actors' platform can be
heard in the uppermost ring of seats. Moreover,
the Greeks spent a great deal of time on music
and voice production. One might almost say that
the whole of Greek drama, from the first line com-
posed by the poet to the last ode sung by the
chorus, was a question of sound: inventing the
right sounds in words and music; keeping them
under trembling control so that as they hit the
ear they seeped into the human heart and there,
slowly and unobtrusively, delineated and refined
the central passion. It was by the sound of his
words as much as by the excellence of his drama—

[9] *Ibid.*

their power and aptness—that a poet moved his audience and so was judged. It was by the delicacy and beauty with which an actor was able to manipulate those sounds that he won his popularity. Voice production was the most important of all the theatrical properties. There is plenty of evidence that actors trained themselves rigorously, fasting and dieting and testing their voices repeatedly before performances and during intervals, to discipline them and bring them into condition.

(16) Was drama spoken or sung?

The dialogue was almost certainly spoken, though there may well have been background music to it. The choral parts, except where the chorus leader joins in the nonlyric dialogue, were sung or chanted.

(17) Do we know anything about the music?

Flutes, drums, cymbals, and trumpets were used, and perhaps occasionally the lyre. However, we know very little about the quality of Greek music, since our knowledge of it (except for a single fragment) begins two hundred years after the time when choral odes were an essential part of drama. There can be no doubt that though the music was important, musical accompaniment was strictly subordinate to the words. "Let the flute follow the dancing revel of the song—it is but an attendant." (Pratinas of Phlius, the great exponent of satyric drama, writing early in the fifth century B.C.)

(18) Is it true that the acting was statuesque and stylized, and that the costumes were grotesque?

It is true that in tragedy the acting was formal, restrained, and seldom violent; but that it was statuesque in the sense of wooden or monolithic is certainly an exaggeration. Though the Greeks were not aiming at realism or naturalism, they *were* aiming at a heightened effect of the real and the natural, something which any kind of excess—especially of the grand manner—would certainly kill. As to the costuming, if one excludes the satyr plays, it was not until a later and decadent period that the grotesque became popular. In its golden age the blend of formality and realism in the Greek theater would hardly have seemed more statuesque to us than grand opera does, or the miming, say, of a Marcel Marceau or a Jean Louis Barrault.

(19) How were the actors able to express their feelings through masks?

The mask stylized the predominant features of a character. Since the characters in a Greek play were not "round," but showed more or less one face to the world, masks could be appropriate and convincing, especially as in such vast theaters personal changes of feature would largely have gone unseen. As to other ways of depicting character, the Greek actor was free to display his feelings through an almost limitless range of gesture, which the Athenians considered of paramount importance: slow and fast movements, kneeling, leaping, lying, turning. If there occurred a momentary discrepancy between what an actor felt and what his mask expressed—some sudden access of grief or joy—he could always hide this by making a movement: turning, embracing, stooping. There must have been changes of mask too: in *Oedipus the King*, for instance, after Oedipus has blinded himself, and in *Hecuba* after the blinding of Polymnestor.

(20) Did the members of the chorus wear masks too?

Probably, and identical masks, though this was by no means always so. In *The Birds* of Aristophanes, for instance, many kinds of birds are represented. When it comes to human types and categories such as age, youth, citizenship, slavery—for example; the Old Men of *The Agamemnon*, the Young Captive Women of *The Eumenides*, the Citizens of Thebes in the *Oedipus Rex*—each would be depicted in different and appropriate masks.

(21) What about the "cothurnos" or thick-soled, high-padded shoes the actors were supposed to have worn?

Scholars differ. Some say that they were among the innovations designed by Aeschylus; others, that they came in only at a later and decadent period. Here is Sir Arthur Pickard-Cambridge: "The theory that actors wore shoes in which the thickness of the soles was increased to four and even eight or ten inches is no longer supported by any scholar of reputation." [10] (But he is referring only to the fifth century B.C.)

[10] *Op. cit.*

(22) What was the composition of the chorus?

Originally the chorus numbered fifty. It was cut down to twelve by Aeschylus,[11] raised to fifteen by Sophocles, and was twenty-four in the satyr plays and comedies of Aristophanes.

The chorus entered the stage to march music and grouped itself in the "orchestra" in a rectangular formation presenting a block of three files and five ranks,[12] with a front of three members, thus:

1	6	11
2	7	12
3	8	13
4	9	14
5	10	15

The dances had a military precision to them, with stately shiftings of the body, ordered gestures, and scant locomotion. The chorus's entries and departures were preceded by the flute player, who might be richly dressed. The entry of the chorus in *The Agamemnon*, with its anapaestic marching measure, is a typical entry of one of the earlier plays. The last fourteen lines of *The Eumenides* are a typical finale. In those plays which have no anapaestic opening for the chorus (*Antigone, Oedipus Rex, Hippolytus, Iphigeneia in Aulis,* and others), the chorus entered perhaps singing the

[11] Though he may occasionally have gone back to the larger number, as is thought in *The Eumenides*.

[12] "Weaker performers were kept in the middle, where they would be less obvious. Thus 'middle row of the chorus' had the derogatory sense which 'back row' had in our musical comedies." From Peter D. Arnott, *An Introduction to the Greek Theatre*. London: Macmillan & Co., Ltd., 1961. By far the soundest and most informative popular exposition I have come upon.

strophes and antistrophes of the parodos (first ode), though it might equally well have entered mute, with the flutist playing a prelude. After that the members of the chorus would take up their positions and face the audience to sing.[18]

(23) What was the function of the chorus?

In the early days of Greek drama, when it was little more than a choral epic with lyric sequences sung by fifty performers, the chorus took almost no part in the action. Later, the occasional dialogue between it and the one actor was simply an interlude in the choric dance. Later still, under Aeschylus, with a chorus cut down to twelve and with two actors, it began to enter the dramatic action itself.

Under Sophocles the chorus retained its importance, but more as an intermediary between the actors (now three) and the audience. It answered the need for someone to represent the "man in the street," who could comment, give information, sum up, and, on occasion, set forth the poet's own views and feelings. In general, the function of the chorus became to underline the action of the plot, comment on the characters, bring out and unify the emotional and moral implications of the story, give relief from tension, and, finally, by its unique means of dance, song, and high-powered poetry, double the emotional involvement of the audience.

All these properties remained true of the chorus under Euripides, but less so. With his modern vision focused on the psychology of men and women

[18] It must be remembered that there was no proscenium curtain.

themselves, the comments of the chorus, whether in dialogue or ode, began to become unnecessary. The choral songs (in their first step toward disappearing altogether) became interludes rather than contributions to the drama.

(24) Did the chorus speak or only sing?

Those parts where the coryphaios (leader of the chorus) joined in the nonlyric dialogue were certainly spoken. At other times (a notable example would be the huddle of old men immediately after the murder of Agamemnon) several members of the chorus spoke individually. As to the odes of the parodos and stasima, these were sung or chanted by the whole chorus in unison. Infinite pains must have been taken with the clear and evocative enunciation of the words. There are no grounds for thinking that the chorus ever *spoke* in unison. All speaking was done either by the chorus leader or by single members.

(25) Do the strophes and antistrophes correspond to a division of the chorus into two semichoruses which answered each other?

This was certainly true of some of the choruses of Aristophanes. As to the other playwrights, scholars differ. Sir Arthur Pickard-Cambridge says there is no evidence for this. On the other hand, it is difficult to see a reason for strophe and antistrophe if some such arrangement did not obtain, although strophe, which means turning, and antistrophe, turning back, could have referred to the pivotal movements of the whole chorus. Beyond this there is no reason to suppose that the chorus repeated its actions in strophe and antistrophe (different words always call for different gestures), though the music probably *was* repeated. As to the events in the play, the members of the chorus must have suited their actions to the drama not only when they were singing the odes but throughout the speeches and movements of the main characters.

(26) Do we know anything about the dances of the Greek chorus?

Little for certain, except that they were stately and restrained and not what we ordinarily mean by "dancing." Music and the dance, however, were considered by the Athenians as the keystones of education. One could not have a healthy mind in a healthy body if that body was dumb to music and movement. Sophocles himself was an accomplished dancer, and as a lad of sixteen danced before the trophy after the Greek victory at Salamis, playing the lyre. He also joined in the girls' ball game on the beach in his own tragedy of *Nausicaa*. We know too that the dance was chiefly mimetic: symbolizing character, emotion, and action through gesture and rhythmic movement. Great use was made of the hands, and of the movements of the body—bending, stooping, turning, swaying —which could express feeling without necessarily any locomotion at all.[14] Peter Arnott, describing

[14] At a later period in Greek history, pantomimic dancing became the most popular form of entertainment.

a modern production of a Greek tragedy at Epidaurus, writes:

> The chorus movements are directed with great
> beauty and skill. Now advancing on the audi-
> ence, now retreating, now crossing the orchestra
> in a diagonal pattern, now draping themselves
> frieze-like along the front of the stage, they main-
> tain an unbroken formal unity against which the
> action proceeds. Their movements echo and
> emphasize the emotions expressed on the stage.
> They cower at moments of fear, raise their arms
> aloft in triumph, swirl apart and come together
> in excitement. The chorus is used not only to
> deliver its own part but as a constant balletic ac-
> companiment of the actors.[15]

This description, I believe, would essentially fit a
tragic chorus of fifth-century Athens.

(27) Was admission to the theater free?

Admission was free at first; later by ticket. In
the time of Demosthenes (fourth century B.C.) a
seat cost 2 obols a day (equivalent to 25 cents or
1/6d). Since it was a civic duty to attend the festivals Pericles established a theater fund (the Theoric
Fund) from which the poor citizens were given
money to buy tickets. A great many of these tickets
or tokens have been unearthed, ranging from the
end of the fifth century B.C. until well on into the
early Christian era. They look rather like coins
and are of bronze, lead, ivory, bone, and terra
cotta. There were special seats for distinguished

[15] *Op. cit.*

persons (as usual, in the most conspicuous and least satisfactory places). It is probable that men and women sat in different parts of the auditorium, and that courtesans sat away from the other women.

(28) At what time of day did the plays begin?

At dawn. The dramatic poet for the day furnished a tetralogy of three tragedies and a satyr play. Finally the day ended with the performance of a comedy by one of the competing comic poets. Since the average time for a tragedy would be about an hour and three-quarters, a satyr play fifty minutes, and a comedy about an hour and fifty minutes, the total time needed for performances would be in the region of between seven and eight hours.

(29) This speaks of a patient and devoted audience!

Not always patient; devoted, yes—or should we say "passionately interested"? They flocked in from other states and towns, and from all over the countryside. The general air at the Great Dionysia or at the Lenaea must have been one of gaiety, expectation, and fiesta, with shops and booths erected everywhere. Many people probably brought their food with them and ate in the theater itself during intervals. Aristotle tells us that they did not even wait for the intervals if the acting was bad. Refreshments were peddled and sold in the theater, and there was time to go home to eat or rest between plays.

(30) How did the spectators endure those hard stone seats?

They brought mats, blankets, pillows. Distinguished guests and patrons were given their own cushions. There seem to have been awnings (at least at a later period) to shelter the two front rows from the sun—which in any case would not be excessive in January and March.

(31) You said the Greek audience was not always patient?

Nor did it try to hide its feelings. There is plenty of evidence of its noisiness both in approval and disapproval. Sometimes the poets themselves received punishment from their audience for real or imagined shortcomings. When Phrynicus brought to the stage the enactment of the recent fall of Miletus to the Persians, the Athenians burst into tears. Then (in typical Greek fashion), they fined him a thousand drachma (about $280 or £100) and forbade him ever to reproduce the drama. On another occasion, Aeschylus, acting in his own play and reciting lines about the goddess Demeter, was physically attacked by his audience, which had decided he was divulging secrets from the Eleusinian mysteries. The Athenians became so enraged that they rushed the stage, and the poet only escaped by taking sanctuary at one of the altars.[16] Later he was brought to trial—and acquitted. At other times actors or poets were forced

[16] The thymele in the center of the orchestra, or the altar in front of the skene.

to retire by the virulence of the audience's hissing, supplemented by the kicking of heels against the seats (which would have made a loud commotion in the days of the wooden seating). On the other hand the audience was quick to show its approval too, and there is evidence that certain playwrights were not above currying favor with it. Menander—the great comic poet of the fourth and third centuries B.C.—once remarked to Philemon (a lesser writer who, nevertheless, had managed to defeat him several times through graft and bribery): "Tell me, Philemon, with absolute frankness: when you beat me don't you blush?"

(32) Do we know which plays of the great dramatists won first prize, and against whom?

In many instances, yes; just as we know a great many of the titles in the vast lost treasury of Greek plays. Aeschylus is reputed to have written some 90 plays, of which we have the titles of more than 80 and the fragments of over 70.[17] He was a success in his lifetime and won first prize thirteen times. Since on each occasion the poet entered four plays and was judged on the set, this means that Aeschylus entered the contest about twenty-two times. Thirteen victories in only twenty-two entries is certainly high success. He had been reigning some twenty-five to thirty years (assuming that the traditional dates are correct, and also that he would not have had four plays ready every single year) when he was defeated by the young Sophocles. However, he went on to win again next year with

[17] But the complete texts of only seven.

his *Seven Against Thebes*. The last time he won, before going off to the court of King Hieron of Syracuse where he died, was with the *Oresteia*.

Sophocles wrote some 123 plays, of which only seven have come down to us. He was a success with the Athenians from start to finish of his career and won 24 times, i.e., more often than Aeschylus and Euripides put together. He pleased the Athenians by giving an impression of restraint and unassailable orthodoxy, and while no less powerful than Aeschylus (who could frighten with his thunderous grandiloquence) he was both more natural and more suggestive. It is interesting to note, however, that he did not win with his greatest extant masterpiece, the *Oedipus Tyrannus*, which was defeated by Philocles, a nephew of Aeschylus.

Euripides, sixteen years younger than Sophocles but dying a year or two before him, seems to have been too psychological and too modern for the fifth-century audience, although in the century after his death he eclipsed his two great rivals in popularity. During his life he won the prize only four times. Of his reputed 90 plays we have 19. Euripides went into voluntary exile toward the end of his life, discouraged, no doubt, by the indifference of the Athenians to his tragedies. After his death in Macedonia at the court of King Archelaus, the Athenians, suddenly aware of what they had lost, gave him the prize for the fifth time.

Aristophanes wrote some 40 plays, of which we have only 11. He won only four first prizes and it is surprising that *The Birds*—perhaps his greatest masterpiece—was placed only second.

(33) Who judged in these dramatic contests?

The judges and their verdicts were arrived at by a complicated combination of election and lot drawing.

(34) Were the plays put on only three times a year and only at Athens?

These were the chief times, but there were others and at other places,[18] especially by the end of the fifth century B.C. Theaters sprang up throughout the Greek world, which had spread in its colonies all over the Mediterranean. After the death of Alexander the Great in 323 B.C. Hellenic culture extended even to the frontiers of India. Actors' guilds began to flourish and touring companies gave performances everywhere on fitted-up stages. Under Alexander, too, the custom had begun of celebrating all festivals with drama. "It is evident," writes Sir Arthur Pickard-Cambridge, "that the drama and music thus circulating throughout the Greek world was the most popular and influential form of culture for several hundred years."[19]

Nor must it be forgotten that besides the set times and places for the exhibition of drama in the fifth century B.C. the poets themselves gave readings of their plays. Indeed, in the ancient world a reading [20] to a select audience was the accepted form of publication. Manuscripts were copied,

[18] But of native drama in other parts of Greece we know very little.

[19] *Op. cit.*

[20] There is a legend that Sophocles (at the age of ninety) hastened his death by giving a reading of *Antigone*.

sold, read, and quoted. Also, plays could be, and were, put on more than once and in more than one place. Aeschylus, for instance, twice visited Sicily and produced his plays in the great theater at Syracuse. After his death the Athenians honored his memory with a decree which granted state backing to anyone who wanted to produce his plays. They were indeed produced (as were those of Sophocles and Euripides—posthumously) and Aeschylus, dead, won still more prizes over living poets.

(35) What happened to the Greek theater after the fifth century B.C.?

It went into a decline. Though there were descendants of both Aeschylus and Sophocles who continued to achieve a certain fame as playwrights, there were no more great tragic poets after the death of Sophocles in 405 B.C. And comedy, too, passed its peak in the life of Aristophanes himself (450-c.385). The only considerable playwright between the fourth and third centuries was Menander. Otherwise, in the post-Alexandrian period (and even before), the significant dramas performed throughout the Hellenistic world were revivals, and chiefly of Euripides (who thus more than redressed his balance with his two great rivals). It is ironic to think that Greek culture never spread so far or so fast as after the fall of Athens. And it went on spreading for several hundred years —long after her miraculous period in art and literature was over. As to drama, it achieved a kind of fertile mediocrity. Tragedies became dull, conventional, and declamatory. Star performers took the place of star poets, and rhetoric became more

important than poetry. Plays degenerated into
"chamber drama" in that the quality of writing
was more fitted for private reading than for public
performance. When Alexandria, rich and new,
became a center of culture in the third century B.C.,
drama did indeed have a final fling, but there is
little or no record of its products. As far as we
can tell, it seems to have been little more than a
sophisticated scholarship exercising itself—self-
consciously—in undramatic techniques.

(36) In producing or directing Greek tragedy
what should be one's endeavor?

To create a unity of form and content so sublime
yet so immediate that its very effulgence moves
people to wonder, apprehension, sympathy, and
tears. Every other consideration—authenticity of
historical setting and theatrical convention—should
be obliterated before the naked impact of idealized
but essential human beings playing out the eternal
emotions of mankind. Therefore, there must be
art without artiness, dignity without aloofness, humanity without familiarity, the natural without
naturalism. Finally, the total expression, in sound
and sight, must glitter with color, pace, simplicity,
and conviction: that is, *be beautiful.*

GLOSSARY OF
NAMES AND PLACES

ADRASTEA: "the Inescapable One"—another name for Nemesis. She punishes presumptuous words and excessive happiness.

AETNA: the famous volcano in Sicily.

AMAZONS: warrior women who inhabited Themiscyra on the southern shores of the Black Sea. They had their right breast burnt off so as to handle the bow better. Any male children they bore were either killed or sent to their fathers (who came from a neighboring nation), but the females were kept to be brought up as warriors.

ANANGKE: Fate or Necessity—from which nothing, not even Zeus, can escape.

ARGOS: city-state in the Peloponnese whose most famous ruler was Agamemnon.

ARGUS: an earth-born giant with eyes all over his head. He was sent by Hera to watch over Io when she was changed into a cow. At Zeus's bidding Hermes put all his eyes to sleep and cut off his head. Hera set his eyes in the tail of her sacred bird, the peacock.

ARIMASPIANS: a people of Scythia who lived on the banks of a river with golden sands. They had but one eye in the middle of their foreheads and waged continual war against the Griffins, who guarded gold.

ATÉ: a daughter of Zeus who personified infatuation and headlong, fatal impetuosity. She walked lightly over men's heads but never touched the ground. Later she became known as the avenger of unrighteousness.

ATLAS: son of a Titan and brother of Prometheus. Because of the part he played in the battle of the Titans with Zeus he was forced by Zeus to hold up the heavens with his hands.

BIBLINE HILLS: a line of hills in Egypt.

BOSPORUS: two straits on the confines of Europe and Asia Minor.

CANOPUS: an island town on the western mouth of the Nile near Alexandria. It was founded by the Spartans and named after the pilot of Menelaus who died there.

CAUCASUS: a mountain of great height between the Black Sea and the Caspian Sea. The inhabitants were said to gather gold into sheepskins.

CERCHNEA: a spring in the marshy forest of Lerna in Argolis.

CHALYBES: a people of Asia Minor near the east coast of the Black Sea. They were workers in iron, and once powerful.

CIMMERIANS: a mythical people mentioned by Homer who dwelt in the furthest west on the ocean. They were enveloped in perpetual cloud and darkness. Elsewhere they are said to preside at the entrance of Hades. The historical Cimmerians (whom Aeschylus is referring to) lived on the Palus Maeotis (Sea of Azov) in the Chersonese (Crimea).

CISTHENE: a town of Lycia in Asia Minor.

COLCHIS: a province of Asia east of the Black Sea, celebrated on account of the golden fleece and the expedition of the Argonauts. It was the birthplace of Medea. Now Mingrelia.

CRONUS: the youngest son of Uranus and Gaea (Heaven and Earth). He mutilated and overthrew his father; then with the assistance of his family of Titans he made himself sovereign of the world. He took to wife his sister Rhea. Their children were Hestia, Demeter, Hera, Hades, Poseidon, and Zeus. Because his mother prophesied that one of his offspring would overthrow him, he swallowed them all except Zeus. When Zeus grew up he forced Cronus to disgorge his other children, and wrested from him the rule of heaven and earth.

DODONA: the oracle of Zeus in Epirus, in the north of Greece. The will of Zeus was ascertained from the rustling of the leaves of the sacred oaks.

ETHIOPS: a mythical river somewhere between Egypt and Ethiopia.

EPAPHUS: son of Zeus Ammon and Io. The builder of Memphis in Egypt.

FURIES: the same as the Erinyes: of indefinite number but later limited to three: Allecto, Tisiphone, and Megaera. They were females of semimonstrous form who punished every transgressor of the natural order. They were especially hard on murder, perjury, and inhospitality, and could pursue their victims into the other world. Later, they appear of softer aspect (though still stern) and the Athenians changed their names to Eumenides, "The Kindly Ones."

GORGONS: the three terrifying sisters who dwelt on the farthest shores of Ocean in the neighborhood of Night and the Hesperides. Their names were Stheno, Eurale, and Medusa—who was mortal, but their queen. With hair and girdles of snakes, and bloodshot eyes, they could turn men to stone by merely being seen.

GRIFFINS: fabulous animals with the head and wings of an eagle and the body and hindquarters of a lion. They inhabited Scythia and guarded its gold—especially against the Arimaspians.

HADES: son of Cronus and Rhea. He was king of the Underworld. With Persephone he ruled over the shades of the dead, who were conducted to the nether regions by Hermes. Hades also came to be the name of the Underworld itself.

HEPHAESTUS: the Latin Vulcan, the lame god of fire and the forge: patron of all the arts dependent on the use of fire.

HERA: the Roman Juno—Queen of Heaven and the sister and jealous wife of Zeus.

HESIONE: daughter of Laomedon, a king of Troy whom Heracles slew because of a broken promise. Hesione was given to Telamon and bore him a son called Teucer, who became the best archer among the Greeks in their seige of Troy.

HYBRISTES: a river in the north of Asia Minor flowing between the Black Sea and the Caucasus.

IO: beautiful daughter of Inachus and priestess of
Hera at Argos. Zeus fell in love with her and
Hera changed her into a white heifer out of
jealousy. When Argus of the hundred eyes
(who had been set to watch her) had been
killed through Zeus's instigation, Hera sent
a gadfly to pursue her in perpetuity.

INACHUS: ancient king of Argos and father of Io.
Originally god of the river Inachus and son
of Oceanus and Tethys.

LERNA: a marsh and forest near the sea in the south-
west of the Argolic plain. It was once the
haunt of the nine-headed hydra slain by Heracles. Through Lerna flowed a stream.

MAEOTIS: part of the sea between Saia and Europe
at the north of the Euxine. Now the Sea of
Azov.

MOIRA: the goddess of Fate who spun the thread
of life for men at their birth. Later there were
three: Clotho (the spinner), Lachesis (dis-
poser of lots), and Atropos (the inevitable
one who cuts the thread).

MOLOSSIA: a region in Epirus (northern Greece)
named from King Molossus, son of Andro-
mache and Pyrrhus.

NILOTIS: city on the banks of the Nile.

OCEANUS: Son of Uranus and Gaea (Heaven and
Earth). Father of seas, rivers, streams, fountains. He was the ancient river of the world
which flows round and bounds the earth and
is itself unbounded. As a deity he came to be
represented as a gentle and hospitable old man
with a flowing beard and crabs' horns.

OLYMPUS: mountain in Thessaly nearly 10,000 feet
high. Zeus had his throne on the summit. The

other "Olympian" gods and goddesses lived in the ravines, lesser peaks, and valleys.

URANUS: Heaven, the son and husband of Gaea, Earth, from whose union sprang the Titans. He would not let his children see the light but buried them deep under the earth. Enraged at this, Gaea stirred up her children against him, and Cronus, the youngest, unmanned him.

PHORCIDES: the Gorgons and Graeae, daughters of Phorcus, an ancient sea-god. Here Aeschylus means the three Graeae, who were born with gray hair and passed their one eye and one tooth from one to the other. They were the protectresses of the Gorgons.

PLUTO: not to be confused in this context with the Roman Pluto, who was Hades. This Pluto was a minor deity called: "Giver of Riches."

POSEIDON: brother of Zeus; god of the sea and all things liquid. With his trident he stirred the oceans and opened fountains.

PROMETHEUS: "the Forethinker." Son of the Titan Iapetus and the ocean nymph Clymene; also brother of Atlas and Epimetheus ("Afterthought") and father of Deucalion. Aeschylus makes him son of Themis—by whom he is put in touch with all the secrets of the future. As the champion of mankind he is punished by Zeus for insubordination.

PYTHO: Pythoness, the Pythia: the prophetess of Apollo at Delphi.

RHEA: wife and sister of Cronus; mother of Zeus. She managed to prevent Cronus from swallowing Zeus at his birth by bearing him in a cavern on the island of Crete and giving Cronus a stone to swallow instead of the infant. She was known as the mother of the gods.

SALMYDESSUS: a city and bay on the Black Sea.

SCYTHIANS: general designation for the nomadic peoples of the vast regions of Scythia: Russia, Hungary, Germany, Scandinavia, Poland, etc.

TARTARUS: a dark abyss which lay as far below the earth as the earth was beneath the heavens. It served as the prison for Cronus and the dethroned Titans. Later it was identified with the lower reaches of Hades where the damned suffered torment.

TETHYS: wife of Oceanus; the original mother. The two together lived gently and hospitably in the farthest west, away from the world's doings.

THEMIS: goddess of law and order and divine justice; also protector of the oppressed.

THEMISCYRA: home of the Amazons on the southern shores of the Black Sea.

THERMODON: river in the country of the Amazons, flowing into the Black Sea.

TITANS: children of Uranus and Gaea: six sons and six daughters. Incited by their mother, they rebelled and overthrew Uranus, establishing their brother Cronus as king. The grandchildren of Uranus and Gaea were known as Titans too, one of whom was Prometheus. Later when Cronus was in turn overthrown by his son, Zeus, the majority of the Titans sided with Zeus. Those who did not were hurled down into Tartarus.

TYPHO: a giant or monster whom Zeus struck with lightning and buried under Mount Aetna.

ZEUS: son of Cronus and Rhea. He dethroned his father and became the supreme lord of the gods and men.